CHINESE EUNUCHS

Books LLC®, Reference Series, Memphis, USA, 2011. ISBN: 9781156074428. www.booksllc.net. Copyright: http://creativecommons.org/licenses/by-sa/3.0/deed.en

Table of Contents

Chinese eunuchs
Huang Hao 1
Li Lianying 2
Sun Yaoting 2
Tong Guan 2
Zhao Gao 3
Zong Ai 4
Zuo Feng 5

Han Dynasty eunuchs
Cai Lun 5
Sima Qian 6
Sun Cheng 8
Zheng Zhong 9

Ming Dynasty eunuchs
Eight Tigers 9
Gang Bing 9
Hong Bao 10
Liu Jin 11
Nguyen An 11
Wang Jinghong 11
Wang Zhen (eunuch) 11
Wei Zhongxian 12
Yishiha 12
Zheng He 13
Zhou Man 19

Tang Dynasty eunuchs
Cheng Yuanzhen 20
Gao Lishi 21
Li Fuguo 25
Qiu Shiliang 27
Tian Lingzi 30
Tutu Chengcui 33
Wang Shoucheng 34
Yang Fugong 36
Yang Fuguang 38
Yu Chao'en 39
Zhu Jingmei 41

Introduction

Purchase of this book entitles you to a free trial membership in the publisher's book club at www.booksllc.net. (Time limited offer.) Simply enter the barcode number from the back cover onto the membership form. The book club entitles you to select from hundreds of thousands of books at no additional charge. You can also download a digital copy of this and related books to read on the go. Simply enter the title or subject onto the search form to find them.

Each chapter in this book ends with a URL to a hyperlinked online version. Type the URL exactly as it appears. If you change the URL's capitalization it won't work. Use the online version to access related pages, websites, footnotes, tables, color photos, updates. Click the version history tab to see the chapter's contributors. Click the edit link to suggest changes.

A large and diverse editor base collaboratively wrote the book, not a single author. After a long process of discussion and debate, the chapters gradually took on a neutral point of view reached through consensus. Additional editors expanded and contributed to chapters striving to achieve balance and comprehensive coverage. This reduced the regional or cultural bias found in many other books and provided access and breadth on subject matter otherwise little documented.

Huang Hao

This is a Chinese name; the family name is Huang.

Huang Hao was a eunuch serving Liu Shan, second and last emperor of the Kingdom of Shu during the Three Kingdoms era in ancient China. Highly favoured by Liu Shan, he was commonly blamed for misguiding the latter into surrendering to the Kingdom of Wei and considered one of the most corrupt and worthless officials in the Three Kingdoms era along with Cen Hun.

Huang Hao entered the service of Liu Shan as a eunuch some time in the 220s. According to the *Chronicles of the Three Kingdoms*, Huang Hao was favoured by Liu Shan as he was shrewd and full of flattering words. While the chief attendant to the emperor Dong Yun was still alive, he often advised Liu Shan on the danger of flattery on one hand, and admonished Huang Hao for misguiding the young emperor on the other.

After Dong Yun died in 246, he was replaced by Chen Qi, who collaborated with Huang Hao to influence court affairs. Henceforth Huang Hao became increasingly powerful. Even the senior ministers such as Zhuge Zhan and Dong Jue could do nothing to remove him. The General-in-Chief, Jiang Wei, once advised Liu Shan to execute Huang Hao since Huang easily fell for a ruse by Wei's Sima Yi to spread false rumours about Jiang wanting to rebel and told the emperor, which resulted in Jiang retreating back into the capital despite the initial victories against Sima Yi. However the emperor denied the request, saying that the eunuch was but a servant who ran errands. Fearing retaliation, Jiang Wei then left the capital of Chengdu to garrison troops at Tazhong (沓中, northwest of present day Zhouqu County, Gansu). As he had not achieved any significant gain over the Kingdom of Wei for years, Jiang Wei was also almost replaced by the another general Yan Yu (閻宇), at the suggestion of Zhuge Zhan and Huang Hao, who was close friends with Huang.

In 263, Jiang Wei wrote to Liu Shan, warning about the mustering of Wei troops under Zhong Hui near the border. However, Huang Hao, who believed in witchery, had a witch predict the future and told Liu Shan that the enemy would take ages to arrive as the capital Chengdu was surrounded by a perfect natural barrier of mountains and valleys. Liu Shan then neglected Jiang Wei's defence plans which ultimately resulted in the capture of Chengdu by Deng Ai's forces. After Liu surrendered, Huang Hao was captured by Deng who intended to execute the treacherous man. However, Huang Hao managed to bribe those close to Deng Ai and extricate himself. His fate henceforth is unknown. (In Chapter 119 of the 14th century historical novel *Romance of the Three Kingdoms* Huang Hao was eventually executed publicly at the order of Sima Zhao when he followed Liu Shan into the capital Luoyang.)

Source (edited): "http://en.wikipedia.org/wiki/Huang_Hao"

Li Lianying

Li Lianying (simplified Chinese: 李连英; traditional Chinese: 李連英; pinyin: *Lǐ Liányīng*; November 12, 1848 - March 4, 1911) was an imperial eunuch during the Qing Dynasty who rose to power during the rule of Empress Dowager Cixi, who was the de facto ruler of China for thirty-nine years from 1869–1908. He served as the Head Eunuch (总管太监) until getting deposed in 1908. Li Lianying was known to be dominant in court affairs, controlling everything from the actions of other eunuchs, to which officials could be granted an audience by the Empress Dowager. Such things often involved large amounts of bribery, and Li Lianying made a fortune from it.

Miscellaneous

The 1991 film *Li Lianying: The Imperial Eunuch*, directed by Tian Zhuangzhuang presents a portrait of Li Lianying.

Source (edited): "http://en.wikipedia.org/wiki/Li_Lianying"

Sun Yaoting

Sun Yaoting (Traditional Chinese: 孫耀庭, Simplified Chinese: 孙耀庭, Hanyu Pinyin: Sūn Yàotíng, Wade-Giles: Sun Yao-t'ing; December 29, 1902 – December 17, 1996) was the last surviving imperial eunuch of Chinese history.

Source (edited): "http://en.wikipedia.org/wiki/Sun_Yaoting"

Tong Guan

This is a Chinese name; the family name is Tong.

Tong Guan (1054–1126), style name **Daofu** (道夫), was a Chinese court eunuch, military general, political adviser, and Council of State to Emperor Huizong of the Song Dynasty. In the *Water Margin*, one of the Four Great Classical Novels of Chinese literature, Tong Guan is featured as an antagonist and enemy of the 108 Liangshan outlaws. He appears mainly in the later chapters.

Life and career

Tong Guan began his military career under the mentorship of a leading eunuch general of the 1080s, becoming one of many eunuch generals found during the Song period. Despite being a eunuch, it was written by many that Tong had strong personal character and was in peak physical condition, with a long beard that was considered unusual for eunuchs. Tong gained his first military victory in battle during the year of 1104, Emperor Huizong granted him a valuable document of his own calligraphy, written in his unique "slender gold" style. After Tong gained reputation by commanding a series of victorious battles in the northwest against the Tanguts, he became the favorite military general and advisor of Emperor Huizong. In the year 1111 he accompanied a diplomatic mission to the Liao Dynasty to the northeast, and after this his career steadily advanced. In 1112 he was promoted to the top of the military command structure and by 1116 he was the first eunuch in Song times to gain entry into the top echelons of central administration as one of the chief policymakers. Tong was involved in all of the elite social gatherings of the time, as his name appeared as a guest on numerous lists for organized parties and banquets hosted by Emperor Huizong. He was also one of only ten palace eunuchs who had their biographies as painters compiled and written for the court.

In the year 1118, Tong suggested to Emperor Huizong that a military alliance with the Jurchens would be favorable in crushing the Liao once and for all. Emperor Huizong agreed, despite some protest by other ministers at court. In a secret alliance and mission of envoys across the borders, Tong played a leading role in the agreement that was reached between the Jurchens and the Song government to divide Liao's territory (while the Song would ultimately obtain their coveted prize: the Sixteen Prefectures). In 1120, at the age sixty-six, Tong was put in command of an army to begin the assault on the Liao state's southern capital at Yanjing. However, the campaign was halted for a time when word came to Tong's camp that a revolt had broken out within the Song Empire, the Fang La Rebellion in Zhejiang province. His army was forced to march several hundred miles south to Zhejiang in order to suppress this rebellion. After successfully quelling this rebellion, his army marched back north but was routed in battle. Shortly after this, the Jurchens defeated the Liao at Yanjing and occupied the city. The city of Yanjing was turned over to Song forces only after a substantial payment was made to the Jurchens. Due to his losses and inability to take Yanjing, when Tong returned to the Song capital at Kaifeng he was forced to retire from his post as commander.

Although earlier forced to retire, in 1124 Tong was called back into military service by Huizong, who trusted no other general more than Tong to head the mission across the northern border. However, in the last month of 1125, Tong fled across the border back to Kaifeng to deliver the ill-fated news that the Jurchens had begun an invasion of Song China. Tong was made the leader of Huizong's personal bodyguard after Huizong abdicated the throne and fled from Kaifeng. Tong was later blamed for much of the disaster that befell Song when the Jurchens conquered northern China. Huizong's successor Emperor Qinzong had Tong Guan executed.

Source (edited): "http://en.wikipedia.org/wiki/Tong_Guan"

Zhao Gao

Zhao Gao (traditional Chinese: 趙高; died 207 BC) was the chief eunuch during the Qin Dynasty of China. He played an instrumental role in the downfall of the Qin Dynasty.

Early life
Zhao Gao was distantly related to the ruling house of the state of Zhao. According to the Shiji, Zhao Gao's parents committed crimes and were punished. Both Zhao Gao and his brother were made eunuchs. However Qin Shi Huang valued Zhao Gao since he was an expert in law and punishment. This was very useful to Qin Shi Huang since he himself was always looking for ways to control the people by laws and punishments. Zhao Gao enjoyed a steady rise in position.

When Zhao was a minor official, he committed a crime punishable by death. Meng Yi was the official in charge of sentencing and he sentenced Zhao to death and removed him from the officials list as instructed by Qin Shi Huang. Zhao was later pardoned by Qin Shi Huang and returned to his official status.

Coup following Qin Shi Huang's death
At the end of the reign of the First Emperor, Qin Shi Huang, Zhao was involved in the death of Marshal Meng Tian and his younger brother Meng Yi. Meng Tian, a reputable general and a supporter of the Emperor's oldest son Fusu, was stationed at the northern border, commanding more than 100,000 troops for the inconclusive campaign against the Huns. Following the sudden death of Qin Shi Huang at the Shaqiu prefecture, Zhao and the Imperial Secretariat Li Si persuaded the emperor's second son Huhai to falsify the emperor's will. The fake decree forced Fusu to commit suicide and stripped Meng Tian of his command. Mindful of hatred for the previous sentencing by Meng Yi, Zhao destroyed the Meng brothers by issuing a false decree of Huhai, now the Second Emperor. He forced Meng Tian to commit suicide and also had Meng Yi killed.

Qin Er Shi, who viewed Zhao Gao as his teacher, became the next Qin emperor.

Zhao Gao also killed Li Si, ironically executing him via the "The Five Pains" method, Li's own invention. The method consisted of having the victim's nose cut off, cutting off a hand and a foot, then the victim was castrated and finally cut in half in line with the waist. He also executed Li Si's family down to the third generation.

In 207 BC, rebellions rose one after another across China. Zhao was afraid that the Second Emperor might make him responsible for the uprisings. To preempt this, Zhao forced the emperor to commit suicide and installed his nephew, Fusu's son Ziying as the new emperor. (Note: Some scholars pointed out that Fusu's son might be too young to plot the demise of Zhao Gao and Ziying might be a brother of the First Emperor instead.)

Ziying soon killed Zhao and surrendered to Liu Bang. The Qin Dynasty collapsed, three years after the death of Qin Shi Huang, and less than twenty years after it was founded.

One Chinese idiom that is derived from an incident involving Zhao is "calling a deer a horse" (traditional Chinese: 指鹿為馬; pinyin: *zhǐ lù wéi mǎ*). In that incident, Zhao, in order to completely control the government, devised a test of loyalty of the officials. Once, at a formal imperial gathering, he brought a deer in front of the officials and called it a horse. Naturally, Qin Er Shi disagreed, but thought Zhao was joking. Some officials followed the emperor's lead, while some followed Zhao's lead. Zhao then took steps to eliminate the officials who refused to call the deer a horse. In later idiomatic usage, the term refers to a deliberate untruth for ulterior motives.

Alternative viewpoints

There is a conspiracy theory that Zhao Gao was a descendant of the royal family of the Kingdom of Zhao, which was destroyed by Qin, and Zhao Gao was seeking revenge on Qin. With Zhao Gao in charge of the Qin government, it was natural that the Qin Empire collapsed in such a short time. In fact, Zhao Gao killed all the sons and daughters of Qin Shi Huang, including the Second Emperor, Huhai. In revenge, Ziying killed Zhao Gao and all of his family members. Thus Zhao Gao or his brothers have no known descendants.

Li Kaiyuan (李開元), a historian from China, believes Zhao Gao was not a eunuch at all. He bases this in part on the fact eunuchs were not allowed to serve as prime minister, which Zhao did.

Source (edited): "http://en.wikipedia.org/wiki/Zhao_Gao"

Zong Ai

Zong Ai (宗愛) (died 452) was a eunuch who briefly came to great power in the Chinese/Xianbei dynasty Northern Wei in 452 after assassinating Emperor Taiwu and making his son Tuoba Yu emperor.

Little is known about Zong's career prior to 451. What is known is that he was punished with castration for unspecified crimes, and subsequent to his castration, he served in the Northern Wei palace as a eunuch. In spring 451, when Emperor Taiwu held a great gathering of imperial officials and handed out titles and other rewards for officials' accomplishments, Zong was created the Duke of Qing Commandery, but it is not known for what accomplishments he was created as such.

Later in 451, Zong came into conflict with Emperor Taiwu's crown prince Tuoba Huang. Crown Prince Huang had been considered able and all-seeing, but overly trusting of his associates, while privately managing farms and orchards and receiving profits from them. Crown Prince Huang greatly disliked Zong, who was described as corrupt and power hungry, and Zong decided to act first, accusing Crown Prince Huang's associates Chou'ni Daosheng (仇泥道盛) and Ren Pingcheng (任平城) of crimes, and Chou'ni and Ren were executed. Further, many other associates of Crown Prince Huang were dragged into the incident and executed. Crown Prince Huang himself grew ill in anxiety, and died in summer 451. Soon, however, Emperor Taiwu found out that Crown Prince Huang was not guilty, and became heavily regretful of his actions in pursuing the crown prince's associates.

Fearful that he would be punished because of Crown Prince Huang's death, Zong assassinated Emperor Taiwu in spring 452. Initially, the officials Wuluolan Yan (烏洛蘭延), Suhe Pi (素和跋), and Chigan Ti (叱干提) did not announce news of Emperor Taiwu's death, as they considered whom to make Emperor Taiwu's successor. Because they considered Crown Prince Huang's son Tuoba Jun to be too young and wanted an older emperor, they summoned Emperor Taiwu's second son, Tuoba Han (拓拔翰) the Prince of Dongping to the palace. However, their discussions stalemated when Chigan insisted on making Tuoba Jun, who as the crown prince's older son would be the proper heir under the Confucian rules of succession, emperor. Zong heard this, and believing that he had already offended Tuoba Jun and disliking Tuoba Han, he secretly summoned Emperor Taiwu's youngest son Tuoba Yu, the Prince of Nan'an, to the palace, while forging an edict from Emperor Taiwu's wife Empress Helian to summon Wuluolan and a number of other officials, who did not suspect that anything was wrong and entered the palace. Upon their doing so, 30 eunuchs that Zong had armed arrested and executed them, as well as Tuoba Han. Zong then made Tuoba Yu emperor. Zong was created the Prince of Fengyi and made the commander of the armed forces, and he became the actual power in the regime.

In fall 452, displeased at how powerful and arrogant Zong had become, Tuoba Yu planned to strip him of his authority. Zong heard about this, and while Tuoba Yu was making a sacrifice to his great-grandfather Emperor Daowu at night, Zong sent his assistant Jia Zhou (賈周) to assassinate him. He then considered whom to make emperor to replace Tuoba Yu, quickly rejected a suggestion by his associate Dugu Ni to make Tuoba Jun emperor, on the account that Tuoba Jun, once he was grown, would surely make Zong account for his father's death. Dugu then entered into a plot with other officials, Yuan He, Baba Kehou (拔拔渴侯), and Buliugu Li and rose against Zong, seizing him and making Tuoba Jun emperor. Both Zong and Jia were executed by extremely cruel means—a five step process:

- Their faces were tattooed.
- Their noses were cut off.
- Their big toes were cut off.
- They were killed by repetitive whipping.
- Their bodies were decapitated, and then the bodies were ground up.

Zong's and Jia's clans were also slaughtered.

Subsequent historians have pondered the unusual natures of Zong's crimes—that despite having assassinated two emperors, Zong was only accused by the coup leaders of having assassinated Tuoba Yu, not Emperor Taiwu. The officials' failure to arrest Zong or to announce Emperor Taiwu's death also led to speculation that Zong did not act alone. However, insufficient information is available to judge whether the speculations are correct.

Source (edited): "http://en.wikipedia.org/wiki/Zong_Ai"

Zuo Feng

Zuo Feng was a eunuch who lived during the Eastern Han Dynasty. According to the Romance of the Three Kingdoms, Zuo Feng had Lu Zhi arrested on trumped up charges after Lu Zhi failed to pay Zuo bribe during the Yellow Turban Rebellion.

Source (edited): "http://en.wikipedia.org/wiki/Zuo_Feng"

Cai Lun

This is a Chinese name; the family name is Cai.

Cai Lun (simplified Chinese: 蔡伦; traditional Chinese: 蔡倫; pinyin: ***Cài Lún***; Wade–Giles: **T'sai Lun**) (ca. 50 AD – 121), courtesy name **Jingzhong** (敬仲), was a Chinese eunuch. He is traditionally regarded as the inventor of paper and the papermaking process, in forms recognizable in modern times as paper (as opposed to Egyptian papyrus). Although paper existed in China before Cai Lun (since the 2nd century BC), he was responsible for the first significant improvement and standardization of paper-making by adding essential new materials into its composition.

Life

Cai Lun (蔡伦) was born in Guiyang (modern day Leiyang, Hunan) during the Eastern Han Dynasty. After serving as a court eunuch from AD 75, he was given several promotions under the rule of Emperor He of Han. In AD 89 he was promoted with the title of *Shang Fang Si*, an office in charge of manufacturing instruments and weapons; he also became a Regular Palace Attendant (中常侍). He was involved in palace intrigue as a supporter of Empress Dou, and in the death of her romantic rival, Consort Song. After the death of Empress Dou in AD 97, he became an associate of Consort Deng Sui.

In AD 105, Cai invented the composition for paper along with the papermaking process - though he may have been credited with an invention of someone from a lower class. Tools and machinery of papermaking in modern times may be more complex, but they still employ the ancient technique of felted sheets of fiber suspended in water, draining of the water, and then drying into a thin matted sheet. For this invention Cai would be world-renowned posthumously, and even in his own time he was given recognition for his invention. A part of his official biography written later in China read thus (Wade-Giles spelling):

In ancient times writings and inscriptions were generally made on tablets of bamboo or on pieces of silk called chih. But silk being costly and bamboo heavy, they were not convenient to use. Tshai Lun Cai Lun then initiated the idea of making paper from the bark of trees, remnants of hemp, rags of cloth, and fishing nets. He submitted the process to the emperor in the first year of Yuan-Hsing [+105] and received praise for his ability. From this time, paper has been in use everywhere and is universally called 'the paper of Marquis Tshai'.

As listed above, the papermaking process included the use of materials like bark, hemp, silk, and fishing net; his exact formula has been lost. Emperor He was pleased with the invention and granted Cai an aristocratic title and great wealth.

In 121, Consort Song's grandson Emperor An of Han assumed power after Empress Deng's death and Cai was ordered to report to prison. Before he was to report, he committed suicide by drinking poison after taking a bath and dressing in fine silk robes. Will Durant, The Story of Civilization: Our Oriental Heritage, Chapter XXV-The Age of the Artists, part 2 (The Revival of Learning) Cai was later revered in Chinese ancestor worship. Fei Zhu of the later Song Dynasty (960-1279) wrote that a temple in honor of Cai Lun had been erected in Chengdu, where several hundred families involved in the papermaking industry traveled five miles from the south to come and pay respects.

Influence

The creator of this extremely important invention is only somewhat known outside East Asia. After Cai invented the papermaking process in 105, it became widely used as a writing medium in China by the 3rd century. It enabled China to develop its civilization (through widespread literature and literacy) much faster than it had with earlier writing materials (primarily bamboo and silk).

By the 7th century, China's papermaking technique had spread to Korea, Vietnam, and Japan. In 751, some Chinese paper makers were captured by Arabs after Tang troops were defeated in the Battle of Talas River. The techniques of papermaking then spread to the West. When paper was first introduced to Europe in the 12th century, it gradually revolutionized the manner in which written communication could be spread from region to region. Along with contact between Arabs and Europeans during the Crusades (with the essential recovery of ancient Greek written classics), the widespread use of paper aided the foundation of the Scholastic Age in Europe.

Source (edited): "http://en.wikipedia.org/wiki/Cai_Lun"

Sima Qian

Sima Qian

Sima Qian (ca. 145 or 135 BC – 86 BC), also called **Ssu-ma Ch'ien**, was a Prefect of the Grand Scribes (太史公) of the Han Dynasty. He is regarded as the father of Chinese historiography because of his highly praised work, *Records of the Grand Historian* (史記 or 史记), a "Jizhuanti" style general history of China covering more than two thousand years from the Yellow Emperor to Emperor Han Wudi (漢武帝 or 汉武帝). His definitive work laid the foundation for later Chinese historiography.

Early life and education

Sima Qian was born and grew up in Longmen, near present-day Hancheng, Shaanxi. He was raised in a family of astrologers. His father, Sima Tan, served as the Prefect of the Grand Scribes of Emperor Wu of Han (Emperor "Han Wudi"). His main responsibilities were managing the imperial library and maintaining or reforming the calendar. Due to the intensive training given by his father, by the age of ten, Sima Qian was already well versed in old writings. He was the student of the famous Confucians Kong Anguo (孔安國 or 孔安国) and Dong Zhongshu. At the age of twenty, with the support of his father, Sima Qian started a journey throughout the country, collecting useful first-hand historical records for his main work, *Shiji*. The purpose of his journey was to verify the ancient rumors and legends and to visit ancient monuments, including the renowned graves of the ancient sage kings Yu and Shun. Places he had visited include Shandong, Yunnan, Hebei, Zhejiang, Jiangsu, Jiangxi and Hunan.

After his travels, he was chosen to be a Palace Attendant in the government whose duties were to inspect different parts of the country with Emperor Han Wudi. In 110 BC, at the age of thirty-five, Sima Qian was sent westward on a military expedition against some "barbarian" tribes. That year, his father fell ill and could not attend the Imperial Feng Sacrifice. Suspecting his time was running out, he summoned his son back to complete the historical work he had begun. Sima Tan wanted to follow the *Annals of Spring and Autumn* - the first chronicle in the history of Chinese literature. Fueled by his father's inspiration, Sima Qian started to compile *Shiji* in 109 BC. In 105 BC, Sima was among the scholars chosen to reform the calendar. As a senior imperial official, Sima was also in the position to offer counsel to the emperor on general affairs of state.

Portrait of Sima Qian

In 99 BC, Sima Qian became embroiled in the Li Ling Affair: Li Ling and Li Guangli (李廣利), two military officers who led a campaign against the Xiongnu in the north, were defeated and taken captive. Emperor Han Wudi attributed the defeat to Li Ling, and all the officials in the government condemned Li Ling for the defeat. Sima was the only person to defend Li Ling, who had never been his friend but whom he respected. Emperor Han Wudi interpreted Sima's defence of Li Ling as an attack on his brother-in-law, who had also fought against the Xiongnu without much success, and sentenced Sima to death. At that time, execution could be commuted either by money or castration. Since Sima did not have enough money to atone his "crime", he chose the latter and was then thrown into prison, where he endured three years. He described his pain thus: "When you see the jailer you abjectly touch the ground with your forehead. At the mere sight of his underlings you are seized with terror... Such ignominy can never be wiped away."

In 96 BC, on his release from prison, Sima chose to live on as a palace eunuch so as to complete his histories, rather than commit suicide as was expected of a gentleman-scholar. As Sima Qian's words explained:

> " The losses he [Li Ling] had formerly inflicted on the enemy were such that his renown filled the Empire! After his disgrace, I was ordered to give my opinion. I extolled his merits, hoping the Emperor would take a wider view, but ...in the end it was decided I was guilty of trying to mislead the Emperor...
> I had not the funds to pay a fine in lieu of my punishment, and my colleagues and associates spoke not a word in my behalf. Had I chosen suicide, no one would have credited me with dying for a principle. Rather, they would have thought the severity of my offense allowed no other way out. It was my obligation to my father to finish his his- "

torical work that made me submit to the knife...If I had done otherwise, how could I have ever had the face to visit the graves of my parents?

...There is no defilement so great as castration. One who has undergone this punishment is nowhere counted as a man. This is not just a modern attitude; it has always been so. Even an ordinary fellow is offended when he has to do business with a eunuch -- how much more so, then, a gentleman! Would it not be an insult to the court and my former colleagues if now I, a menial who sweeps floors, a mutilated wretch, should raise my head and stretch my eyebrows to argue right and wrong?

I am fit now for only guarding the palace women's apartments. I can hope for justification only after my death, when my histories become known to the world."

Historian

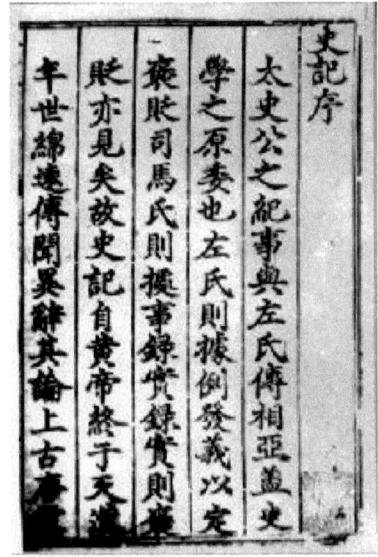

The first page of *Shiji*.

Although the style and form of Chinese historical writings varied through the ages, *Shiji* has defined the quality and style from then onwards. Before Sima, histories were written as certain events or certain periods of history of states; his idea of a general history affected later historiographers like Zheng Qiao (鄭樵) in writing Tongshi (通史) and Sima Guang (司馬光) in writing Zizhi Tongjian (資治通鑑). The Chinese historical form of dynasty history, or Jizhuanti history of dynasties, was codified in the second dynastic history by Ban Gu's (班固) History of Han (漢書), but historians regard Sima's work as their model, which stands as the "official format" of the history of China.

In writing *Shiji*, Sima initiated a new writing style by presenting history in a series of biographies. His work extends over 130 chapters — not in historical sequence, but was divided into particular subjects, including annals, chronicles, treatises — on music, ceremonies, calendars, religion, economics, and extended biographies. Sima's influence on the writing style of histories in other places is also evident in, for example *The History of Korea*.

Literary figure

Sima's *Shiji* is respected as a model of biographical literature with high literary value, and still stands as a "textbook" for the study of classical Chinese worldwide. Sima's works were influential to Chinese writing, serving as ideal models for various types of prose within the neo-classical ("renaissance" 復古) movement of the Tang-Song (唐宋) period. The great use of characterisation and plotting also influenced fiction writing, including the classical short stories of the middle and late medieval period (Tang-Ming), as well as the vernacular novel of the late imperial period.

The influence is derived from the following key elements of his writing:

Skillful depiction

Sima portrayed many distinguished subjects based on true historical information. He would illustrate the response of the subject by placing him in a sharp contrast or juxtaposition, and then letting his words and deeds speak for him. The use of conversations in his writing also makes the descriptions more vibrant and realistic.

Innovative approach

Sima's new approach in writing involved using language that was informal, humorous and full of variations. This was an innovative way of writing at that time and thus it has always been esteemed as the highest achievement of classical Chinese writing; even Lu Xun (魯迅) regarded *Shiji* as "the unique work of all historians, the songs of Qu Yuan without rhyme." (史家之絕唱, 無韻之離騷) in his Hanwenxueshi Gangyao (《漢文學史綱要》).

Concise language

The style was simple, concise, fluent, and easy-to-read. Sima made his own comments while recounting the historical events. In writing the biographies in *Shiji*, he avoided making general descriptions, and instead tried to catch the essence of the events. He would portray the subjects concretely, giving the readers vivid images with strong artistic appeal.

Other literary works

Apart from *Shiji*, Sima wrote a famous letter to his friend Ren An, in which expressed his suffering during the Li Ling Affair and his perseverance in writing *Shiji*. This letter is a highly admired example of literary prose style and is widely studied in China even down to the present. Sima Qian had written eight rhapsodies (*Fu* 賦), which are listed in *Hanshu* bibliographic treatise. All but one of these have been lost. The only one to survive, the "Rhapsody in Lament for Gentleman who do not Meet their Time" 士不遇賦, is probably not complete.

Astrologer

Sima and his father were both court astrologers (*taishi*) 太史 in the Former Han Dynasty. At that time, the astrologer had an important role, responsible for interpreting and predicting the course of government according to the influence of the Sun, Moon, and stars, as well as other phenomena like solar eclipses, earthquakes, etc.

Before compiling *Shiji*, in 104 BC, Sima Qian created *Taichuli* (太初曆), which can be translated as 'The first calendar') on the basis of the Qin calendar. Taichuli was one of the most advanced calendars of the time. The creation of Taichuli was regarded as a revolution in the Chinese calendar tradition, as it stated that there were 365.25 days in a year and 29.53 days in a month.

Sima adopted a new method in sorting out the historical data and a new approach to writing historical records. He analyzed the records and sorted out those that could serve the purpose of *Shiji*. He intended to find out the patterns and principles of the development of human history.

Sima emphasised the role of men in affecting the historical development of China. It is the first time in Chinese history that men were put under the spotlight in the analysis of historical development. He also denounced Emperor Han Wudi, who was superstitious, and prayed to gods extravagantly. In addition, he also proposed his historical perception that a country cannot escape from the fate of the boom-bust cycle. With these in-depth analyses and insight, Sima set an example for writing journalistic articles in later generations.

Unlike *Hanshu*, which was written under the supervision of the Imperial Dynasty, *Shiji* was a privately written historiography. Although Sima was the Prefect of the Grand Scribes in the Han government, he refused to write *Shiji* as an official historiography covering only those of high rank. The work also covers people of the lower classes and is therefore considered a "veritable record" of the darker side of the dynasty.

The minor planet 12620 Simaqian is named in his honour.

Books about Sima Qian in English

- Burton Watson (1958) *Ssu-ma Ch'ien: Grand Historian of China*. New York: Columbia University Press.
- Yang Hsien-yi and Gladys Yang (1974), *Records of the Historians*. Hong Kong: Commercial Press.
- Sima, Qian and trans. Watson, Burton (1993), *Records of the Grand Historian: Han Dynasty*. Research Center for Translation, The Chinese University of Hong Kong and Columbia University Press.
- Sima, Qian and trans. Watson, Burton (1993), *Records of the Grand Historian: Qin Dynasty*. Research Center for Translation,

Source (edited): "http://en.wikipedia.org/wiki/Sima_Qian"

Sun Cheng

Sun Cheng (孫程) (died 132) was an eunuch during Han Dynasty who, contrary to the stereotypes of Han eunuchs being corrupt and power-hungry, was loyal to the imperial family and tried (unsuccessfully) to counter the culture of corruption.

Contribution to Emperor Shun's restoration

During Emperor An's reign, his various trusted person, including the eunuchs Jiang Jing (江京) and Li Run (李閏) and his wet nurse Wang Sheng (王聖), as well as his wife Empress Yan Ji, effectively ran the imperial administration, and they used this opportunity to corruptly seize for themselves power and wealth. One of the things Jiang and Empress Yan engaged in was to, in 124, falsely accuse the nine-year-old Crown Prince Liu Bao (劉保) of crimes and getting Emperor An to depose him and make him the Prince of Jiyin.

In 125, Emperor An died suddenly, and even though Prince Bao was Emperor An's only son, Empress Yan wanted someone younger to control, and so she made Liu Yi (劉懿), the Marquess of Beixiang, emperor.

When the young emperor became gravely ill later in the year, Sun, who was then a mid-level eunuch, became concerned that Empress Dowager Yan would again bypass Prince Bao, the rightful heir, and so he entered into a conspiracy with a number of other eunuchs. They swore an oath to restore Prince Bao, and several days after the former Marquess of Beixiang died, they made a sudden assault on the palace and welcomed Prince Bao to the palace and proclaimed him emperor (as Emperor Shun). After several days of battling with the empress dowager's faction, the eunuchs led by Sun prevailed, and the Yan clan was slaughtered.

For their contributions to his restoration, Emperor Shun created Sun and 18 of his fellow eunuchs marquesses.

Failed attempt to guide Emperor Shun onto the right path

Emperor Shun, whose disposition was generally meek but weak, quickly himself became controlled by those eunuchs and officials around him, who were largely corrupt. Sun despised this situation, and in 126, when the eunuch Zhang Fang (張防) was accused of corruption by the governor of the capital district, Yu Xu (虞詡) but instead turned the situation around and convinced Emperor Shun that Yu had falsely accused him and should be sentenced to death, Sun and another eunuch who helped restore Emperor Shun, Zhang Xian (張賢), interceded at great personal peril to themselves. Yu was spared, while Zhang was exiled. However, officials who were close to Zhang then attacked Sun and his fellow eunuch-marquesses of being overly arrogant. Emperor Shun therefore sent them out of the capital Luoyang, to their marches. Of the 19, Sun alone became sufficiently enraged by this development that he had his marquess seal and emblems returned to the emperor and secretly stayed in the capital, looking to find another chance to try to guide the emperor onto the right path. He was soon captured, but Emperor Shun, remembering his accomplishments, simply sent him back to his march without further punishment, but also without listening to his advice on stamping out corruption.

Later in life

In 128, Emperor Shun, remembering what Sun and the others had done for him, summoned them back to the capital, but largely again ignored their advice. In 132, Sun died and was buried with great honors, including the posthumous name Gang (剛, literally "unbending").

Source (edited): "http://en.wikipedia.org/wiki/Sun_Cheng"

Zheng Zhong

Zheng Zhong (鄭眾), courtesy name **Jichan** (季產) (died 107), was the first Han Dynasty eunuch with true power in government, thanks to the trust that Emperor He had in him for his contributions in overthrowing the clan of Empress Dowager Dou, particularly her autocratic brother Dou Xian. He was also a close associate of Emperor He's wife Empress Deng Sui and continued to be powerful after Emperor He's death, during her regency over his son Emperor Shang and Emperor An. He was also the first Eastern Han Dynasty eunuch to be created a marquess. (The only Western Han Dynasty eunuch who was created a marquess was Empress Xu Pingjun's father Xu Guanghan (許廣漢), whose creation was thanks to his relationship with his daughter and his son-in-law Emperor Xuan, not his post as a eunuch.)

Zheng was from Nanyang Commandery (roughly modern Nanyang, Henan) -- the same commandery that the Eastern Han imperial clan was from. He was described to be cautious, agile, and a deep thinker. He first served in the household of Emperor Zhang while he was still crown prince under his father Emperor Ming. After Emperor Zhang ascended the throne, he was eventually promoted to the post of imperial attendant (中常侍).

During the time of Empress Dowager Dou's regency over Emperor He, Zheng served as the director of imperial gardens (鉤盾令). He was one of the eunuchs who did not endear himself to Empress Dowager Dou's clan. In 92, Emperor He, apparently dissatisfied with his suppression by the Dou clan, plotted a coup d'état with his brother Liu Qing the Prince of Qinghe, and Zheng. They were successful in carrying out the overthrow of the Dous, and as a reward, Emperor He promoted Zheng to the post of the empress' palace's head of household (大長秋). Zheng accepted the post but declined most of the monetary rewards that Emperor He gave him, a fact that made Emperor He even more impressed with him. Emperor He often consulted with him on major affairs of state, and this started a precedent of eunuchs becoming involved in imperial governance.

In 102, breaking past precedent, Emperor He created Zheng the Marquess of Chaoxiang.

Zheng supported Emperor He's wife Empress Deng through the turmoils of Emperor He's death in 106 and the death of his son and successor Emperor Shang later that year. For his support, she added 300 households to his march in 107. He died later that year.

Source (edited): "http://en.wikipedia.org/wiki/Zheng_Zhong"

Eight Tigers

The **Eight Tigers** (Chinese: 八虎; pinyin: *Bā Hǔ*), sometimes referred to as the "Gang of Eight" (八党/八黨), were a powerful group of eunuchs that controlled the Chinese imperial court during the reign of the Ming Dynasty Zhengde Emperor (r. 1505-1521 CE).

Led by Liu Jin (刘瑾) the remaining members of the coterie were Ma Yongcheng (马永成/馬永成), Gao Feng (高凤/高鳳), Luo Yang (罗祥), Wei Bin (魏彬), Qiu Ju (丘聚), Yu Dayong (谷大用) and Zhang Yong (張永/张永).

Source (edited): "http://en.wikipedia.org/wiki/Eight_Tigers"

Gang Bing

Gang Bing (simplified Chinese: 刚秉; traditional Chinese: 剛秉; pinyin: *Gāng Bǐng*; Wade–Giles: Kang Ping) was a Chinese general and eunuch who served under Emperor Yongle of the Ming Dynasty.

Self-castration

General Gang Bing is most notable for his act of self-castration as a display of loyalty to his emperor. He served under Emperor Yongle, the third emperor of the Ming Dynasty who ruled over China from 1402 to 1424. Historical accounts describe the brave and loyal General Gang Bing as Yongle's favorite general. Because of this Yongle placed Gang Bing in charge of the palace in Beijing while he left for a hunting expedition.

At this point political intrigue within the walls of the Forbidden City forced Gang Bing to make a drastic choice. The Emperor possessed a large harem of concubines; sexual contact with a concubine by anyone other than the emperor was a severe offense. Fearing that rivals within the palace may accuse him of sexual improprieties with one of the seventy three imperial concubines, Gang Bing decided to execute a plan of terrible self-infliction the night before the emperor left for his trip: he severed his own penis and testicles with a knife. The general then placed his severed organs into a bag under the saddle of the emperor's horse.

As predicted, when Yongle returned from his hunt one of the emperor's ministers reported that Gang Bing had had inappropriate relations within the royal harem. When accused of misconduct Gang Bing instructed that the emperor's saddle be retrieved and requested that the emperor reach inside the bag under the saddle. Inside the emperor found Gang Bing's shriveled, blackened genitalia. Deeply impressed, Yongle elevated Gang Bing to the rank of chief eunuch, a politically powerful position within the palace; gave him numerous gifts; and proclaimed him holy.

Memorial

After Gang Bing's death around 1410 Yongle had his general and chief eunuch deified as Patron Saint of Eunuchs. In addition, the emperor assigned a plot of land on the outskirts of Beijing as a cemetery for eunuchs and built an ancestral hall in Gang Bing's honor. In 1530 the ancestral hall was expanded and renamed *The Ancestral Hall of the Exalted Brave and Loyal* (Huguo Baozhong Si), but the temple was popularly known as the "Eunuch's Temple." In the early 20th century the hall was still in use by eunuchs and the temple grounds contained courts and halls. In 1950, after the Communist take over of China, the Eunuch's Temple was renamed *Beijing Municipal Cemetery for Revolutionaries* and in 1970 was again renamed Babaoshan National Cemetery for Revolutionaries, the name it bears today.

Source (edited): "http://en.wikipedia.org/wiki/Gang_Bing"

Hong Bao

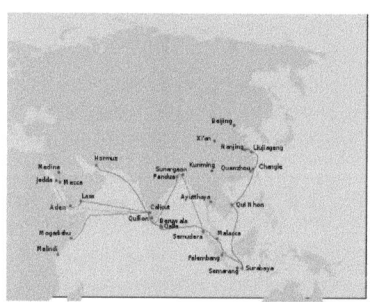

The 7th voyage of Zheng He's fleet. A possible route of Hong Bao's squadron is shown as a dashed line, based on analysis by Edward L. Dreyer.

Hong Bao (Chinese: 洪保; *fl.* ca. 1412-1433) was a Chinese eunuch sent on overseas diplomatic missions during the reign of Ming emperors Yongle and Xuande. He is best known as the commander of one of the detached squadrons of Zheng He's fleet during the Seventh Voyage of this fleet to the Indian Ocean (1431–1433).

Early career

According to the *History of Ming*, in 1412 (i.e., some time between the third and fourth voyages of Zheng He's fleet), Hong Bao was sent by the Yongle Emperor as the envoy to Thailand.

In 1421 Hong Bao participated in the sixth voyage of Zheng He, during which foreign envoys were transported back to their countries, as far as Ormus.

Hong Bao on the Seventh Voyage of Zheng He

Hong Bao's name appears in the inscription made by Zheng He in Liujiagang in 1431, before his fleet left China on its 7th (and last) voyage to the "Western Ocean" (Indian Ocean). According to the inscription, the two Principal Envoys (正使) sent by the Xuande Emperor to the countries of the Western Ocean were the eunuchs Zheng He and Wang Jinghong. Hong Bao was one of the five Assistant Envoys (正使) (along with Zhu Liang, Zhou Man, Yang Zhen, and Zhang Da). Hong Bao, as well as all other Principal and Assistant Envoys except for Zhang Da, had the eunuch rank of Grand Director (太監, *Taijian*).

Much of what we know about Hong Bao comes from the book written by the interpreter Ma Huan, who served in his squadron during the 7th voyage of Zheng He's fleet. According to Edward L. Dreyer's analysis of the preserved sources about the voyage, in particular Ma Huan's book, Hong Bao commanded a squadron which most likely separated from the main fleet in Semudera in northern Sumatra (although other suggested it may have happened earlier, in Qui Nhon in Champa), and visited Bengal. From Bengal, Hong Bao's squadron would then go to Calicut (in southern India), to which the main fleet came directly from Semudera across the Bay of Bengal.

While the main fleet left Calicut to Ormus (in Persian Gulf), Hong Bao's squadron went from Calicut to various destinations on the west side of the Arabian Sea in southern Arabia and Horn of Africa, including Aden and Mogadishu. Before leaving Calicut, Hong Bao sent seven of his sailors, including Ma Huan, to Mecca and Medina aboard a native (Indian?) ship going to Jedda.

Grave

In June 2010, the Chief of Archaeology Department at Nanjing Museum Wang Zhigao announced that a Ming Dynasty grave recently found near Zutang Mountain (祖堂山) in the Jiangning District of Nanjing was identified as that of Hong Bao (and not of Zheng He himself, as it was earlier surmised).

In fiction

In his book *1421: The Year China Discovered the World*, amateur historian Gavin Menzies claims Hong Bao made voyages to Antarctica and Australia.

Source (edited): "http://en.wikipedia.org/wiki/Hong_Bao"

Liu Jin

Liú Jǐn (simplified Chinese: 刘瑾; traditional Chinese: (劉瑾) (? -1510) was a well-known Chinese eunuch during the reign of the Chinese Ming Dynasty Zhengde Emperor (r. 1505-1521). Liu was famous for being one of the most corrupt officials in Chinese history and the emperor in all but name for some time. He was the leader of the "Eight Tigers", a powerful group of eunuchs who controlled the imperial court.

Plotting against the emperor

The Zhengde Emperor 's dissolute lifestyle placed a heavy burden on the people of the empire. He would refuse to receive all his ministers and ignored all their petitions whilst sanctioning the growth of the eunuch community in the imperial palace. Liu made some reforms such as encouraging widows to remarry, a move which went against the Neo-Confucianism views of the time. Many officials and other eunuchs opposed Liu - the uprising of Prince Zhu Zhifan (安化王朱真鐇) was a failed attempt to assassinate Liu and seize power. After officials suppressed the uprising an official called Yang Yiqing (楊一清) persuaded another eunuch Zhang Yong (张永/張永) to report Liu's plotting of rebellion. The Zhengde Emperor did not believe this report at first but took it seriously enough to consider expelling Liu to Fengyang County (凤阳县/鳳陽縣) in Anhui Province but Zhang's discovery of many weapons in Liu's houses sealed his fate.

Death

The emperor ordered Liu executed by death by a thousand cuts over a period of three days, a process that resulted in Liu being cut 3,357 times. According to witnesses, onlookers in Beijing bought his flesh for one qian (the smallest available currency at the time) and consumed it accompanied with rice wine. Liu died on the second day of his punishment after three to four hundred cuts.

Personal wealth

According to one report, shortly before Liu was executed, 12,057,800 taels (449,750 kg) of gold and 259,583,600 taels (9,682,470 kg) of silver were taken from his residence. In 2001, the Asian Wall Street Journal placed Liu on its list of the fifty wealthiest persons in the past 1,000 years although the actual amount may in fact have been lower.

Source (edited): "http://en.wikipedia.org/wiki/Liu_Jin"

Nguyen An

Nguyen An (died 1453), also known as **Ruan An** or **Juan An** (depending on the transliteration system), was a Ming Dynasty eunuch, architect, and hydraulic specialist between the first and fifth decades of the 15th century. Born in Vietnam, he was taken as tribute from Vietnam to China and later became a eunuch and architect in service to the Chinese emperors. He, along with numerous architects, such as master designers and planners Cai Xin (蔡信), Chen Gui (陳珪), and Wu Zhong (吳中), master carpenter Kuai Xiang (蒯祥), and master mason Lu Xiang (陸祥), was an important principal designer and a chief builder of the Forbidden City in Beijing.

Under the reign of Zhengtong Emperor, Nguyen An had a major role in the reconstruction of the wall of Beijing. He was also a hydraulic specialist, who was involved in at least three hydraulic projects and had a flawless record. He died in 1453.

Source (edited): "http://en.wikipedia.org/wiki/Nguyen_An"

Wang Jinghong

Wang Jinghong (simplified Chinese: 王景弘; traditional Chinese: 王景弘; pinyin: *Wáng Jǐnghóng*; Wade–Giles: Wang Ching-hung) (died ca. 1434) was a Chinese mariner, explorer, diplomat and fleet admiral, who was deputy to Zheng He on his voyages to Southeast Asia, South Asia, and East Africa, collectively referred to as the travels of "*Eunuch Sanbao to the Western Ocean*" (Chinese: 三保太監下西洋) or "*Zheng He to the Western Ocean*", from 1405 to 1433. He led an eighth voyage to Sumatra but is said to have died in a shipwreck on the way. He was buried at Semarang in Java aged 78.

Source (edited): "http://en.wikipedia.org/wiki/Wang_Jinghong"

Wang Zhen (eunuch)

This is a Chinese name; the family name is Wang.

Wáng Zhèn (王振) was the first Ming Dynasty eunuch with power in the court. The Zhihua Si Temple in Beijing was built in 1443 at his order.

He was killed (possibly by Ming officers) during the Tumu Crisis (also known as the Battle of Tumu Fortress), a disastrous campaign against the Oirat Mongols for which he was responsible.

Wei Zhongxian

Source (edited): "http://en.wikipedia.org/wiki/Wang_Zhen_(eunuch)"

Wei Zhongxian (traditional Chinese: 魏忠賢) (1568 – October 19, 1627) is considered by most historians as the most powerful and notorious eunuch in Chinese history. Originally a hoodlum and gambler, his initial name was **Wei Si** (魏四, literally, *Wei Fourth*). He took the step of becoming a eunuch and entering palace service to escape from his creditors, taking the name **Li Jinzhong** (李进忠). After entering the palace, he got into the service of Madam Ke (客氏), the wet-nurse of the future Ming emperor. The couple began manipulating the Tianqi Emperor, who renamed him Wei Zhongxian. The emperor's favour later gave Wei absolute power over the court.

Wei persecuted anyone who opposed his decisions, resulting in the death and imprisonment of many officials. He later proclaimed himself to be *Nine-Thousand Years* (九千歲) which meant that he was symbolically the second most important person in the country, just after the emperor, who is called the *Ten-Thousand Years* (萬歲). Wei also built many shrines (生祠) and erected god-like statues of himself in them. In 1627, his control of the court ended with the death of the Tianqi Emperor, whose brother and successor promptly eliminated him. He was forced to commit suicide (some sources say executed by strangulation) and his corpse was disembowelled.

Source (edited): "http://en.wikipedia.org/wiki/Wei_Zhongxian"

Yishiha

Yishiha (Chinese: 亦失哈; Wade-Giles: **Ishiha** or **I-shih-ha**; also **Isiha**) (fl. 1409–1451) was a eunuch in the service of the Ming Dynasty emperors of China who carried out several expeditions down the Sungari and Amur Rivers, and is credited with the construction of the only two Ming Dynasty Buddhist temples ever built on the territory of today's Russia.

Early life

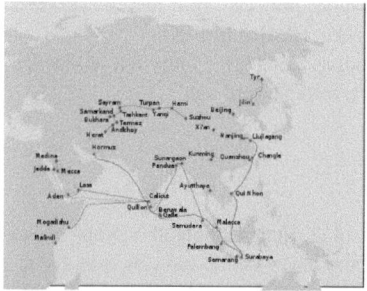

Yishiha's voyages in the context of the Yongle era military and diplomatic activity. Yishiha's route is in blue, along with those of Zheng He (in black) and Chen Cheng (in green)

It is believed that Yishiha was a Haixi Jurchen by origin, and was captured by the Chinese forces in the late 14th century. He worked under two important eunuchs, Wang Zhen and Cao Jixiang. It is speculated by modern historians that he rose to prominence by participating in the court politics and serving Yongle's concubines of Manchurian (Jurchen) origin.

Amur expeditions

Yishiha's Amur expeditions belong to the same period of the Yongle Emperor's reign (1402–1424) which saw another eunuch admiral, Zheng He, sail across the Indian Ocean, and Chinese ambassadors reach the Timurid capital Herat (in today's Afghanistan) overland. By 1409, Yongle's government, who had already established relations with the Haixi and Jianzhou Jurchens in southern Manchuria, ordered Yishiha to start preparations for an expedition to the lower Amur River region, to demonstrate the power of the Ming Empire to the Nurgal (奴儿干) Jurchen populating the area and induce them to enter into relations with the empire, and to ensure that they would not create trouble for the Ming state when the latter went to war with the Eastern Mongols.

In 1411, after two years of preparations, Yishiha's fleet of 25 ships with 1000 men aboard sailed from Jilin City down the Sungari and into the Amur. The "Nurgal Jurchens" offered little oppositions to Yishiha's expedition. He gave generous gifts to their tribal leaders, and established a "Nurgal Regional Military Commission" (奴儿干都司, *Nu'ergan Dusi*), at the place the Chinese called Telin (特林), near today's village of Tyr in Russia's Khabarovsk Krai. This was the same place where in 1260-1320 the Yuan had the headquarters of their Marshal of the Eastern Campaigns. The commission's authority covered much of the Amur basin, including the shores of the Sungari, Ussuri, Urmi, Muling, and Nen Rivers. Yishiha then returned to the empire, taking with him a tribute-bearing mission of 178 "Nurgal Jurchens".

A pillar on top of the Tyr Cliff, remaining from, apparently, Yishiha's second temple, as seen ca. 1860

In 1413-1414, during his second expeditions to the lower Amur, Yishiha stayed almost a year at Tyr. He built a Buddhist temple (sometimes described as a "monastery") named Yongning Si (永宁寺, the Temple of Eternal Peace) dedicated to Guanyin on the Tyr Cliff, and erected a stele describing his expedition, with the text in Chinese, Mongol, and Jurchen languages. The stele, presently kept in the Arseniev Museum in Vladivostok, described the locals as good archers and fishermen, and their clothes as made of fishskin. According to some evidence (a seal issued by the empire's Ministry of Rites, found in Yilan County, Heilongjiang), in 1413 Yishiha also visited the nearby coast of the Sakhalin Island, and granted Ming titles to a local chieftain.

While no detailed ethnographic data about the "Nurgal Jurchens" has been found in Chinese records, it was, apparently, a collective name for the Tungusic peoples and possibly other groups (e.g. Nivkh) populating the area. As of the mid-19th century, Tyr was a Gilyak (Nivkh) settlement, as attested by a contemporary encyclopedia and the book by E.G. Ravenstein, based on the accounts of the Russian explorers of the 1850s. Another ethnic group native to the Ulchsky District (where Tyr is located) are the Ulch people, a Tungusic people, but their home villages are all located upstream from Tyr.

During the rest of Yongle's reign, Yishiha carried out three more expeditions to Nurgal, while the Nurgal natives sent some more tribute and trade missions to the Ming court.

Yongle's successor (short-lived Hongxi (r. 1424–25), or, more likely, Xuande (r. 1425–35)) continued Yongle's policy toward the "Wild Jurchens". In 1425, the Liaodong regional commissioner, Liu Qing, was ordered to build ships for another expedition down the river, and in 1426 Yishiha sailed again.

Yishiha's last mission was connected to the retirement of the Nurgal chief and the "inauguration" of his son as his successor. Yishiha attended at that event in 1432, presenting the new chief a seal of authority and giving gifts to subordinate chieftains. This time Yishiha's fleet included 50 big ships with 2,000 soldiers, and they actually brought the new chief (who had been living in Beijing) to Tyr. As Yoshiha's first (1413) Yongning Si temple had been destroyed by that time, Yishiha had a second temple of the same name built. According to the modern archaeologists, his second temple was not built at the site of his first temple (as it had been commonly believed), but rather at the site of its ancient predecessor - the Yuan Dynasty Yongning Si temple. As the archaeological research has revealed, the 1413 temple was located some 90 meters to the west of the top of the Tyr Cliff, where Yishiha's 1430s temple (and its Yuan predecessor) were located. A second stele was put next to the second temple. The stele has also survived, and now is also located in Vladivostok Museum.

According to modern historians, Yishiha made the total of nine expeditions to the Lower Amur.

Later career

In the 1430s the Xuande government stopped sending sea and river expeditions, and the naval (or, rather, riverine) career of Yishiha came to an end, as did that of his more famous colleague Zheng He. In 1435 Yishiha was put in charge of the defense of the Liaodong region; he remained at this post for over 15 years. Apparently, his performance during the raids of the Oirad Mongol chief Esen Tayisi was considered unsatisfactory, and some time between 1449 and 1451 his was relieved of his duties. No later traces of him have been found by modern historians.

Source (edited): "http://en.wikipedia.org/wiki/Yishiha"

Zheng He

Zheng He (1371–1435, 鄭和 / 郑和; pinyin: Zhèng Hé), also known as **Ma Sanbao** (馬三寶 / 马三宝) and **Hajji Mahmud Shamsuddin** (Persian: حاجی محمود شمس) was a Muslim Hui-Chinese mariner, explorer, diplomat and fleet admiral, who commanded voyages to Southeast Asia, South Asia, the Middle East, and East Africa, collectively referred to as the *Voyages of Zheng He* or *Voyages of Cheng Ho* from 1405 to 1433.

Life

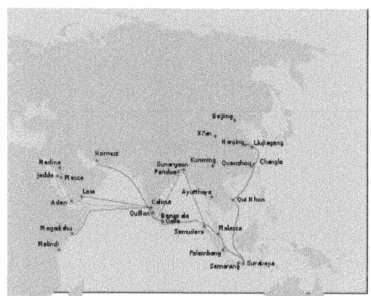

The route of the 7th voyage of Zheng He's fleet. Solid line: main fleet; dashed line: a possible route of Hong Bao's squadron; dotted line: a trip of seven Chinese sailors, including Ma Huan, from Calicut to Mecca on a native ship. Cities visited by Zheng He's fleet or its squadron on the 7th or any of the previous voyages are shown in red.

Zheng, born as **Ma He** (馬和 / 马和), was the second son of a Muslim family which also had four daughters, from Kunyang, present day Jinning, just south of Kunming near the southwest corner of Lake Dian in Yunnan.

He was the great great great grandson of Sayyid Ajjal Shams al-Din Omar, a Persian who served in the administration of the Mongolian Empire and was appointed governor of Yunnan during the early Yuan Dynasty. Both his grandfather and great-grandfather carried the title of Hajji, which indicates they had made the pilgrimage to Mecca. His great-grandfather was named Bayan and may have been a member of a Mongol garrison in Yunnan.

In 1381, the year his father was killed, following the defeat of the Northern Yuan, a Ming army was dispatched to Yunnan to put down the army of the Mongol Yuan loyalist Basalawarmi during the Ming conquest of Yunnan. Ma He, then only eleven years old, was captured by the Ming Muslim troops of Lan Yu and Fu Youde and made a eunuch. He was sent to the Imperial court, where he was called 'San Bao' meaning 'Three Jewels.' He eventually became a trusted adviser of the Yongle Emperor (r. 1403-1424), assisting him in deposing his predecessor, the Jianwen Emperor. In return for meritorious service, the eunuch received the name Zheng He from the Yongle Emperor.

In 1425 the Hongxi Emperor appointed him to be Defender of Nanjing. In 1428 the Xuande Emperor ordered him to complete the construction of the magnificent Buddhist nine-storied Da Baoen Temple in Nanjing, and in 1430 appointed him to lead the seventh and final expedition to the "Western Ocean". Zheng He died during the treasure fleet's last voyage, on the returning trip after the fleet reached Hormuz in 1433.

Expeditions

Between 1405 and 1433, the Ming government sponsored a series of seven naval expeditions. The Yongle emperor designed them to establish a Chinese presence, impose imperial control over trade, impress foreign peoples in the Indian Ocean basin and extend the empire's tributary system. The voyages also presented an opportunity to seek out Zhu Yunwen (the previous emperor whom the Yongle emperor had usurped and who was rumored to have fled into exile) – possibly the "largest scale manhunt on water in the history of China".

Zheng He was placed as the admiral in control of the huge fleet and armed forces that undertook these expeditions. Wang Jinghong was appointed his second in command. Zheng He's first voyage consisted of a fleet of 317 ships (other sources say 200 ships) holding almost 28,000 crewmen (each ship housing up to 500 men).

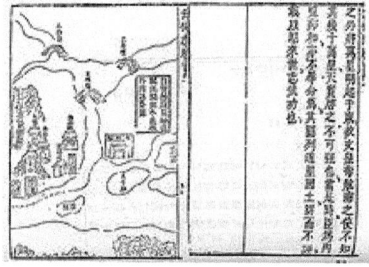

One of a set of maps of Zheng He's missions (郑和航海图), also known as the Mao Kun maps, 1628.

Zheng He's fleets visited Arabia, Brunei, East Africa, India, Malay Archipelago and Thailand (at the time called Siam), dispensing and receiving goods along the way. Zheng He presented gifts of gold, silver, porcelain and silk; in return, China received such novelties as ostriches, zebras, camels, ivory and giraffes.

It is important to note that while the scale of Zheng He's fleet was unprecedented (compared to previous voyages from China to the east Indian Ocean), the routes were not. Sea-based trade links had existed between China and Arabian peninsula since the Han Dynasty (there being trade with the Roman Empire at that time.) During the Three Kingdoms, the king of Wu sent a diplomatic mission along the coast of Asia, reaching as far as the Eastern Roman Empire. During the Song Dynasty, there was large scale maritime trade from China reaching as far as the Arabian peninsula and East Africa. In short, Zheng He's fleet was following long-established, well-mapped routes.

Zheng He generally sought to attain his goals through diplomacy, and his large army awed most would-be enemies into submission. But a contemporary reported that Zheng He "walked like a tiger" and did not shrink from violence when he considered it necessary to impress foreign peoples with China's military might. He ruthlessly suppressed pirates who had long plagued Chinese and southeast Asian waters. For example, he would defeat Chen Zuyi, one of the most feared and respected pirate captains, and return him back to China for execution. He also waged a land war against the Kingdom of Kotte in Ceylon, and he made displays of military force when local officials threatened his fleet in Arabia and East Africa. From his fourth voyage, he brought envoys from thirty states who traveled to China and paid their respects at the Ming court.

In 1424, the Yongle Emperor died. His successor, the Hongxi Emperor (reigned 1424–1425), decided to stop the voyages during his short reign. Zheng He made one more voyage under the Xuande Emperor (reigned 1426–1435), but after that the voyages of the Chinese treasure ship fleets were ended. Zheng He died during the treasure fleet's last voyage. Although he has a tomb in China, it is empty: he was, like many great admirals, buried at sea.

Voyages

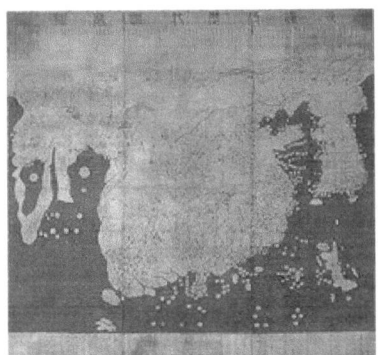

The Kangnido map (1402) predates Zheng's voyages and suggests that he had quite detailed geographical information on much of the Old World.

Zheng He led seven expeditions to what the Chinese called "the Western Ocean" (Indian Ocean). He brought back to China many trophies and envoys from more than thirty kingdoms – including King Vira Alakeshwara of Ceylon, who came to China as a captive to apologize to the Emperor.

The records of Zheng's last two voyages were unfortunately destroyed by the Ming emperor. Therefore it is never certain where Zheng has sailed in these two expeditions. The traditional view is that he went as far as Iran.

Detail of the Fra Mauro map relating the travels of a junk into the Atlantic Ocean in 1420. The ship also is illustrated above the text.

There are speculations that some of Zheng's ships may have traveled beyond the Cape of Good Hope. In particular, the Venetian monk and cartographer Fra Mauro describes in his 1459 Fra Mauro map the travels of a huge "junk from India" 2,000 miles into the Atlantic Ocean in 1420. What Fra Mauro meant by 'India' is not known and some scholars believe he meant an Arab ship. However, Professor Su Ming-Yang thinks "the ship is European, as it is fitted with a crow's nest, or lookout post, at the masthead, and has sails fitted to the yards, unlike the batten sails of Chinese ships."

Zheng himself wrote of his travels:
We have traversed more than 100,000 li (50,000 kilometers or 30,000 miles) of immense water spaces and have beheld in the ocean huge waves like mountains rising in the sky, and we have set eyes on barbarian regions far away hidden in a blue transparency of light vapors, while our sails, loftily unfurled like clouds day and night, continued their course [as rapidly] as a star, traversing those savage waves as if we were treading a public thoroughfare… — Tablet erected by Zheng He, Changle, Fujian, 1432. Louise Levathes

Sailing charts

Part of the chart showing India at top, Ceylon upper right and Africa along the bottom

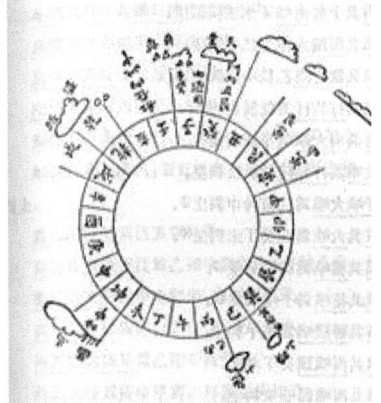

Ming dynasty 24 point compass

Zheng He's sailing charts were published in a book entitled *Wubei Zhi* (Treatise on Armament Technology) written in 1621 and published in 1628 but traced back to Zheng He's and earlier voyages. It was originally a strip map 20.5 cm by 560 cm that could be rolled up, but was divided into 40 pages which vary in scale from 7 miles/inch in the Nanjing area to 215 miles/inch in parts of the African coast.

There is little attempt to provide an accurate 2-D representation; instead the sailing instructions are given using a 24 point compass system with a Chinese symbol for each point, together with a sailing time/distance, which takes account of the local currents and winds. Sometimes depth soundings are also provided. It also shows bays, estuaries, capes and islands, ports and mountains along the coast, important landmarks (pagodas, temples) and shoal rocks. Of

300 named places outside China, more than 80% can be confidently located. There are also fifty observations of stellar altitude.

Size of the ships

Traditional and popular accounts of Zheng He's voyages have described a great fleet of gigantic ships, far larger than any other wooden ships in history. Some modern scholars consider these descriptions to be exaggerated.

Chinese records assert that Zheng He's fleet sailed as far as East Africa. According to medieval Chinese sources, Zheng He commanded seven expeditions. The 1405 expedition consisted of 27,800 men and a fleet of 62 treasure ships supported by approximately 190 smaller ships. The fleet included:

- *Treasure ships* (Chinese:宝船), used by the commander of the fleet and his deputies (nine-masted, about 126.73 metres (416 ft) long and 51.84 metres (170 ft) wide), according to later writers. This is more or less the size and shape of a football field.
- Equine ships (Chinese:馬船), carrying horses and tribute goods and repair material for the fleet (eight-masted, about 103 m (339 ft) long and 42 m (138 ft) wide).
- Supply ships (Chinese:粮船), containing staple for the crew (seven-masted, about 78 m (257 ft) long and 35 m (115 ft) wide).
- Troop transports (Chinese:兵船), six-masted, about 67 m (220 ft) long and 25 m (83 ft) wide.
- Fuchuan warships (Chinese:福船), five-masted, about 50 m (165 ft) long.
- Patrol boats (Chinese:坐船), eight-oared, about 37 m (120 ft) long.
- Water tankers (Chinese:水船), with 1 month's supply of fresh water.

Six more expeditions took place, from 1407 to 1433, with fleets of comparable size.

If the accounts can be taken as factual, Zheng He's treasure ships were mammoth ships with nine masts, four decks, and were capable of accommodating more than 500 passengers, as well as a massive amount of cargo. Marco Polo and Ibn Battuta both described multi-masted ships carrying 500 to 1000 passengers in their translated accounts. Niccolò Da Conti, a contemporary of Zheng He, was also an eyewitness of ships in Southeast Asia, claiming to have seen 5 masted junks weighing about 2000 tons. There are even some sources that claim some of the treasure ships might have been as long as 600 feet. On the ships were navigators, explorers, sailors, doctors, workers, and soldiers along with the translator and diarist Gong Zhen.

Modern study of ship dimensions

A display at the Ibn Battuta Mall in Dubai compares the size of ships used by Zheng He and by Christopher Columbus.

According to recent research by professor of marine engineering Xin Yuanou, the length of many of the ships has been estimated at 59 m (193.6 ft), but is under heavy dispute by other scholars. The East China Jiangsu province announced in 2010 that they were building a replica with a length of 71.1 metres (233 ft), using traditional crafts but with more automation.

The largest ships in the fleet, the treasure ships described in Chinese chronicles, would have been several times larger than any wooden ship ever recorded in history, surpassing *l'Orient* (65 m/213.3 ft long) which was built in the late 18th century. The first ships to attain 126 m (413.4 ft) long were 19th century steamers with iron hulls. Some scholars argue that it is highly unlikely that Zheng He's ship was 450 feet (137.2 m) in length, some estimating that they were 390–408 feet (118.9–124.4 m) long and 160–166 feet (48.8–50.6 m) wide instead while others put them as 200–250 feet (61.0–76.2 m) in length.

One explanation for the seemingly inefficient size of these colossal ships was that the largest 44 Zhang treasure ships were merely used by the Emperor and imperial bureaucrats to travel along the Yangtze for court business, including reviewing Zheng He's expedition fleet. The Yangtze river, with its calmer waters, may have been navigable by these treasure ships. Zheng He, a court eunuch, would not have had the privilege in rank to command the largest of these ships, seaworthy or not. The main ships of Zheng He's fleet were instead 6 masted 2000-liao ships.

Early 17th century Chinese woodblock print, thought to represent Zheng He's ships.

Accounts of medieval travellers

The characteristics of the Chinese ships of the period are described by Western travelers to the East, such as Ibn Battuta and Marco Polo. According to Ibn Battuta, who visited China in 1347:

…We stopped in the port of Calicut, in which there were at the time thirteen Chinese vessels, and disembarked. China Sea traveling is done in Chinese ships only, so we shall describe their arrangements. The Chinese vessels are of three kinds; large ships called chunks (junks), middle sized ones called zaws (dhows) and the small ones kakams. The large ships have anything from twelve down to three sails, which are made of bamboo rods plaited into mats. They are never lowered, but turned according to the direction of the wind; at anchor they are left floating in the wind. Three smaller ones, the "half", the "third" and the "quarter", accompany each large vessel. These vessels are built in the towns of Zaytun and Sin-Kalan. The vessel has four decks and contains rooms, cabins, and saloons for merchants; a cabin has chambers and a lavatory, and can be locked by its occupants. This is the manner after which they are made; two (parallel) walls of very thick wooden (planking) are raised and across the space between them are placed very thick planks (the bulkheads) secured longitudinally and transversely by means of large nails, each three ells in length. When these walls have thus been built the lower deck is fitted in and the ship is launched before the upper works are finished." *(Ibn Battuta)*.

Accounts contemporary to Zheng He's era suggest he was a pious Muslim; these include the writings of Ma Huan, Zheng He's chronicler, interpreter, and fellow Muslim, who travelled with him on many of his voyages. As evidence of Zheng He's high regard for temples and places of worship of other religions, the Galle Trilingual Inscription stone tablet, erected by Zheng He around 1410 in Sri Lanka records details about contributions of gold, silver, and silk that he made on behalf of the emperor at a Buddhist mountain temple. Also, a commemorative pillar at the temple of the Taoist goddess Tian Fei, the Celestial Spouse, in Fujian province records details about his voyages. It has the inscription:

We have traversed more than 100,000 li (50,000 kilometers) of immense water spaces and have beheld in the ocean huge waves like mountains rising in the sky, and we have set eyes on barbarian regions far away hidden in a blue transparency of light vapors, while our sails, loftily unfurled like clouds day and night, continued their course [as rapidly] as a star, traversing those savage waves as if we were treading a public thoroughfare...
—Erected by Zheng He, Changle, Fujian, 1432. Louise Levathes

Indonesian religious leader and Islamic scholar Hamka (1908–1981) wrote in 1961: *"The development of Islam in Indonesia and Malaya is intimately related to a Chinese Muslim, Admiral Zheng He."* In Malacca he built granaries, warehouses and a stockade, and most probably he left behind many of his Muslim crews. Much of the information on Zheng He's voyages was compiled by Ma Huan, also Muslim, who accompanied Zheng He on several of his inspection tours and served as his chronicler / interpreter. In his book 'The Overall Survey of the Ocean Shores' (Chinese: 瀛涯勝覽) written in 1416, Ma Huan gave very detailed accounts of his observations of the peoples' customs and lives in ports they visited. Zheng He had many Muslim Eunuchs as his companions. At the time when his fleet first arrived in Malacca, there were already Chinese Muslims living there. Ma Huan talks about them as *tángrén* (Chinese: 唐人) who were Muslim. At their ports of call, they actively preached Islam, established Chinese Muslim communities, and built mosques.

Zheng Hoo (Zheng He) Mosque. A mosque named after the famous navigator in the Indonesian city of Surabaya

Indonesian scholar Slamet Muljana writes: "Zheng He built Chinese Muslim communities first in Palembang, then in San Fa (West Kalimantan), subsequently he founded similar communities along the shores of Java, the Malay Peninsula and the Philippines. They preached Islam according to the Hanafi school of thought and in Chinese language."

Li Tong Cai, in his book 'Indonesia – Legends and Facts', writes: "in 1430, Zheng He had already successfully established the foundations of the Hui religion Islam. After his death in 1434, Hajji Yan Ying Yu became the force behind the Chinese Muslim community, and he delegated a few local Chinese as leaders, such as trader Sun Long from Semarang, Peng Rui He and Hajji Peng De Qin. Sun Long and Peng Rui He actively urged the Chinese community to 'Javanise'. They encouraged the younger Chinese generation to assimilate with the Javanese society, to take on Javanese names and their way of life. Sun Long's adopted son Chen Wen, also named Radin Pada is the son of King Majapahit and his Chinese wife." It seems likely that Chen Wen is the same Raden Patah, the founder of Demak Sultanate who had a Chinese mother and was a student and/or cousin of Sunan Ampel.

After Zheng He's death, Chinese naval expeditions were suspended. The Hanafi Islam that Zheng He and his people propagated lost almost all contact with Islam in China, and gradually was totally absorbed by the local Shafi'i school of thought. When Melaka was successively colonised by the Portuguese, the Dutch, and later the British, Chinese were discouraged from converting to Islam. Many of the Chinese Muslim mosques became San Bao Chinese temples commemorating Zheng He. After a lapse of 600 years, the influence of Chinese Muslims in Malacca declined to almost nil. In many ways, Zheng He can be considered a major founder of the present community of Chinese Indonesians.

In Malacca

San Bao Temple in Malacaa

According to the Malaysian history, Sultan Mansur Shah (ruled 1459–1477) dispatched Tun Perpatih Putih as his envoy to China and carried a letter from the Sultan to the Ming Emperor. Tun Perpatih succeeded in impressing the Emperor of Ming with the fame and grandeur of Sultan Mansur Shah. In the year 1459, a princess Hang Li Po (or Hang Liu), was sent by the emperor of Ming to marry Malacca Sultan Mansur Shah (ruled 1459–1477). The princess came with her entourage 500 sons of ministers and a few hundred handmaidens. They eventually settled in Bukit Cina, Malacca. It is believed that a significant number of them married into the local populace. The descendants of these mixed marriages are locally known today as Peranakan and still use the honorifics Baba (male title) and Nyonya (female title).

In Malaysia today, many people believe it was Admiral Zheng He (died 1433) who sent princess Hang Li Po to Malacca in year 1459. However there is no record of Hang Li Po (or Hang Liu) in Ming annals. She is mentioned only within Malacca folklore and Malay annals.

Connection to the history of Late Imperial China

A giraffe brought from Somalia in the twelfth year of Yongle (AD 1415).

In the 1950s, historians such as John Fairbank and Joseph Needham popularized the idea that after Zheng He's voyages China turned away from the seas due to the *Hai jin* edict and was isolated from European technological advancements. Modern historians point out that Chinese maritime commerce did not totally stop after Zheng He, that Chinese ships continued to dominate Southeast Asian commerce until the 19th century and that active Chinese trading with India and East Africa continued long after the time of Zheng. The travels of the Chinese *Junk Keying* to the United States and England between 1846 and 1848 testify to the power of Chinese shipping until the 19th century. Moreover revisionist historians such as Jack Goldstone argue that the Zheng He voyages ended for practical reasons that did not reflect the technological level of China.

Although the Ming Dynasty did ban shipping with the *Hai jin* edict, they eventually lifted this ban. By banning oceangoing shipping, the Ming (and later Qing) dynasties had forced countless numbers of people into black market smuggling. This reduced government tax revenue and increased piracy. The lack of an oceangoing navy then left China highly vulnerable to the Wokou pirates that ravaged China in the 16th century.

Richard von Glahn (University of California, Los Angeles Professor of History and a specialist in Chinese history) commented that a majority of school history texts present Zheng He wrongly; they "*offer counterfactual arguments*", and "*emphasize China's missed opportunity.*" The "*narrative emphasizes the failure*" instead of Zheng He's accomplishments. He goes on to claim that "*Zheng He reshaped Asia.*" According to him, maritime history in the fifteenth century is essentially the Zheng He story and the effects of Zheng He's voyages.

Von Glahn claims that Zheng He's influence lasted beyond his age, may be seen as the tip of an iceberg, and there is much more to the story of maritime trade and other relationships in Asia in the fifteenth century and beyond.

State-sponsored Ming naval efforts declined dramatically after Zheng's voyages. Starting in the early 15th century, China experienced increasing pressure from resurgent Mongolian tribes from the north. In recognition of this threat and possibly to move closer to his family's historical geographic power base, in 1421 the emperor Yongle moved the capital north from Nanjing to present-day Beijing. From the new capital he could apply greater imperial supervision to the effort to defend the northern borders. At considerable expense, China launched annual military expeditions from Beijing to weaken the Mongolians. The expenditures necessary for these land campaigns directly competed with the funds necessary to continue naval expeditions.

In 1449 Mongolian cavalry ambushed a land expedition personally led by the emperor Zhengtong less than a day's march from the walls of the capital. In the Battle of Tumu Fortress the Mongolians wiped out the Chinese army and captured the emperor. This battle had two salient effects. First, it demonstrated the clear threat posed by the northern nomads. Second, the Mongols caused a political crisis in China when they released Zhengtong after his half-brother had proclaimed himself the new Jingtai emperor. Not until 1457 did political stability return when Zhengtong recovered the throne. Upon his return to power China abandoned the strategy of annual land expeditions and instead embarked upon a massive and expensive expansion of the Great Wall of China. In this environment, funding for naval expeditions simply did not happen.

Relics

Nanjing Tianfeigong (南京天妃宫)
Zheng He built Tianfeigong (天妃宫, Tianfei palace) in Nanjing after the return of their first western voyage in 1407.

Stele of Tongfan Deed (通番事跡碑)
The stele of Tongfan Deed (通番事跡, deed of foreign connection and exchange) is located in the Tianfeigong in Taicang where they start their journey. It was submerged and disappeared and has been rebuilt.

Stele of Record of Tianfei Showing Her Presence and Power (天妃靈應之記碑)
In order to impetrate and thank the bless of Tianfei, Zheng He and his colleagues rebuilt Tianfeigong at Nanshan, Changle County, Fujian province before their 7th western voyage. They founded a stele with the inscription title Tian Fei Ling Ying Zhi Ji (天妃靈應之記, Record of Tianfei Showing Her Presence and Power) there, which tells about their voyages.

Zheng He Stele in Sri Lanka
Galle Trilingual Inscription in Sri Lanka was discovered in the city of Galle in 1911 and is preserved in the National Museum of Colombo. Three languages were used for inscription: Chinese, Tamil and Persian, which describe his donations to a Buddhist temple, the famous Tenavarai Nayanar temple of Tondeswaram and praises to Allah.

Commemoration

Tomb and museum
Zheng He's tomb in Nanjing has been repaired and a small museum has been built next to it, although his body is missing as he was buried at sea off the Malabar coast near Calicut in Western India. However, his sword and other personal possessions were interred in the typical Muslim tomb inscribed with Arabic characters.

Zheng He's assistant Hong Bao's tomb was unearthed recently in Nanjing.

Maritime Day
In the People's Republic of China, 11 July is Maritime Day (中国航海日) and is devoted to the memory of Zheng He's first voyage.

Gallery

Zheng He's tomb in Nanjing

Museum to honour Zheng He, Nanjing

Zheng He Gallery in Malacca

Zheng He statue in the Quanzhou Maritime Museum

Cultural Influence
In Vernor Vinge's science fiction novel *A Deepness in the Sky*, Qeng Ho, named after Zheng He, is the commercial traders in the human galactical system.

In 2009, China's CCTV released *Zheng He Xia Xiyang*, a television series specially produced in 2005 to mark the 600th anniversary of Zheng He's voyages. Gallen Lo starred as Zheng He.

The expeditions of Zheng He were also featured in the 2005 novel "The Map Thief" by Heather Terrell.

Source (edited): "http://en.wikipedia.org/wiki/Zheng_He"

Zhou Man

This is a Chinese name; the family name is Zhou.

A display at the Ibn Battuta Mall in Dubai compares the size of ships used by Zheng He and by Christopher Columbus. The larger is a model of a Zheng He treasure ship.

Zhou Man (Chinese: 周滿; pinyin: *Zhōu Mǎn*), was a 15th century Chinese admiral and explorer. He was born into a wealthy merchant family in the year 1378 AD; when he was six years old, his father died on an overseas voyage to Korea. Mourning his father's death, he left his mother and his four younger siblings behind. He worked his way into the emperor's staff by the age of 22. At 32, he was assigned "Grand Leader of All Vessels Commanded by the Emperor's Swift Hand."

Zhou, with the help of three other commanders, explored wide reaches of the Indian Ocean. A stone inscription, dated 1431, at the Palace of the Celestial Spouse in Liujiagang, Jiangsu is translated as:

We, Zheng He and his companions [including Admirals Hong Bao, Zhou Man, Zhou Wen, and Yang Qing], at the beginning of Zhu Di's reign received the Imperial Commission as envoys to the barbarians. Up until now seven voyages have taken place and, each time, we have commanded several tens of thousands of government soldiers and more than a hundred ocean-going vessels. We have...reached countries of the Eastern Regions, more than thirty countries in all. We have...beheld in the ocean huge waves like mountains rising sky-high, and we have set eyes on barbarian regions far away, hidden in a blue transparency of light vapors, whilst our sails, loftily unfurled like clouds, day and night continued their course, rapid like that of a star, traversing those savage waves.

In fiction

Thomas Seinbeck's " In the Shade of the Cypress" is a historic novel, the main historic Character is Zhou Man. Published 2010

In his book *1421: The Year China Discovered the World*, amateur historian Gavin Menzies claimed that Zhou Man's fleet approached and mapped the Pacific coast of North America. According to Menzies, his fleet might be wiped out by a Megatsunami caused by a Meteorite creating Mahuika crater.

Source (edited): "http://en.wikipedia.org/wiki/Zhou_Man"

Cheng Yuanzhen

Cheng Yuanzhen (程元振) (died 764?) was a eunuch official of the Chinese dynasty Tang Dynasty. He was exceedingly powerful early in the reign of Emperor Daizong and was said to, in his attempts to consolidate his power, have killed or demoted a number of key generals and officials on his own whim, and thus drew the hatred from the other officials and generals. In 763, he was blamed for not warning Emperor Daizong about the Tufan invasion that eventually caused the capital Chang'an to fall to Tufan forces, forcing Emperor Daizong to flee. Emperor Daizong exiled him, and he died in exile.

Background

Cheng Yuanzhen was from Jingzhao Municipality (京兆) -- the special municipality centered around the Tang capital Chang'an. He was a eunuch from his youth and served at the eunuch bureau (內侍省, *Neishi Sheng*), eventually rising to be the commander of the imperial guard archer corps (內射生使, *Nei Shesheng Shi*) as well as the deputy director of the imperial stables, under the powerful eunuch Li Fuguo, late in the reign of Emperor Suzong.

Rise to power

In summer 762, Emperor Suzong was seriously ill, near death. By this point, Emperor Suzong's wife Empress Zhang, who was previously allied with Li Fuguo, was no longer allied with him, and she tried to enter into an alliance with Emperor Suzong's son (not her son) the crown prince Li Yu, to kill Li Fuguo and Cheng Yuanzhen and seize power. Li Yu declined, and she then entered into an alliance with Li Yu's younger brother Li Xi (李係) the Prince of Yue, trying to lay a trap for Li Fuguo (and possibly Li Yu). When she issued an edict in Emperor Suzong's name summoning Li Yu, Cheng found out about her plan and detained Li Yu, escorting him to the imperial guard headquarters. He and Li Fuguo then led troops into the palace and arrested Empress Zhang and Li Xi. Upon Emperor Suzong's death, Li Fuguo executed Empress Zhang, Li Xi, and Li Xian (李僩) the Prince of Yan, and then declared Li Yu emperor (as Emperor Daizong).

For two months early in Emperor Daizong's reign, Li Fuguo was exceedingly powerful, so much so that he was telling Emperor Daizong not to bother with any thing and just let him handle the matters of state, and Emperor Daizong gave him chancellor title, as well as several other honorific titles. Cheng was made a commanding general of the imperial guards, but was not satisfied, as he wanted to take over Li Fuguo's power, and therefore he secretly plotted with Emperor Daizong. With cooperation from Cheng, later in summer 762, Emperor Daizong, while creating Li Fuguo a prince, stripped Li Fuguo of his military command and transferred it to Cheng. Li Fuguo was subsequently assassinated on Emperor Daizong's orders, and Emperor Daizong and Cheng governed together.

It was said that Cheng was suspicious and jealous of the senior generals and officials and did what he could to strip them of power. For example, he was jealous of Guo Ziyi and often criticized him before Emperor Daizong, leading Guo, who was fearful of the situation, to resign his command and remain at Chang'an. When the senior official Pei Mian had disagreements with Cheng, Cheng had Pei demoted to the remote Shi Prefecture (施州, roughly modern Enshi Tujia and Miao Autonomous Prefecture, Hubei). Meanwhile, he sometimes made requests of the general Lai Tian (來瑱) -- the military governor (*Jiedushi*) of Shannan East Circuit (山南東道, headquartered in modern Xiangfan, Hubei), which Lai rejected, and thus he was resentful of Lai. In 763, while Lai was at Chang'an, he and his associate Wang Zhongsheng (王仲升), who was also resentful of Lai, jointly falsely accused Lai of treason. Lai was exiled and, on the way to exile, was ordered to commit suicide. Cheng also disliked the major general Li Guangbi and often submitted reports against Li Guangbi. The general Li Huairang (李懷讓), the military governor of Tonghua Circuit (同華, headquartered in modern Weinan, Shaanxi), was also falsely accused by Cheng and committed suicide in fear in 763. It was said that given these incidents, all of the generals felt insecure and alienated from the imperial government. Despite this, Cheng was still arrogant and believed that he could grab more power.

Downfall

Throughout the spring and summer of 763, Tufan forces were progressively attacking and capturing Tang prefectures to the west of Chang'an. It was said that despite the generals' urgent requests for aid, Cheng Yuanzhen did not relay the requests to Emperor Daizong. By winter 763, Tufan forces were approaching Chang'an; only then did Emperor Daizong realize the seriousness of the Tufan threat and commission Guo Ziyi to resist Tufan. When Emperor Daizong issued an edict to the various circuits ordering emergency aid, however, the generals refused to respond, and Guo could not quickly gather troops large enough to resist Tufan forces. Emperor Daizong was forced to abandon Chang'an and flee to Shan Prefecture (陝州, in modern Sanmenxia, Henan).

The imperial officials who followed Emperor Daizong to Shan Prefecture blamed the disaster on Cheng—in both his failure to alert Emperor Daizong as to the seriousness of the Tufan threat and his alienation of the generals, causing a lack of aid to arrive. The imperial scholar Liu Kang (柳伉) submitted a harshly worded petition, asking that Cheng be executed. Emperor Daizong, however, remembering how Cheng had protected him in the past, declined to do so. He did, however, remove Cheng from his offices and order that he return home.

When Emperor Daizong returned to Chang'an around the new year 764, Cheng heard the news. Putting on women's clothing in disguise, he secretly entered Chang'an and plotted to return to power. He was arrested by the Jingzhao Municipality government, and the imperial censors subsequently submitted an indictment against him. In spring 764, Emperor Daizong exiled him to Zhen Prefecture (榛州, in modern Chongqing), but soon changed the location of exile to the more prosperous city of Jiangling. Cheng died there, in exile, shortly after arriving there.

Source (edited): "http://en.wikipedia.org/wiki/Cheng_Yuanzhen"

Gao Lishi

Gao Lishi (traditional Chinese: 高力士; pinyin: *Gāo Lìshì*) (684–762), formally the **Duke of Qi** (齊公), was a eunuch official of the Chinese dynasty Tang Dynasty and Wu Zetian's Zhou Dynasty, becoming particularly powerful during Emperor Xuanzong of Tang's reign. He is believed to have been in charge of many decisions that were supposed to be the emperor's responsibility during Emperor Xuanzong's later years, and was believed to have been richer than many of the nobility of the era. Despite this, however, he was often viewed as a positive example of eunuch participation in politics for his personal loyalty to Emperor Xuanzong, which withstood despite its putting himself in personal danger later, during the reign of Emperor Xuanzong's son Emperor Suzong (when Emperor Xuanzong was *Taishang Huang* (retired emperor)) as it drew jealousy from fellow eunuch Li Fuguo. Further, during the years of his highest power, he was also said to make no improper influences on governance, and therefore drew no anger from the intelligentsia. Late in Emperor Suzong's reign, he was exiled upon Li Fuguo's urging. After a pardon in 762, he was returning from exile, when he heard of Emperors Xuanzong's and Suzong's deaths. Mourning Emperor Xuanzong bitterly, he grew ill and died.

Background

Gao Lishi was born in 684, when Empress Dowager Wu (later known as Wu Zetian) was successively regent over her sons Emperor Zhongzong (Li Zhe/Li Xian) and Emperor Ruizong (Li Dan). He was from Pan Prefecture (潘州, roughly modern Maoming, Guangdong). His original family name was Feng (馮), and he was reportedly a great-grandson of the early Tang local government official Feng Ang (馮盎). In 698, a local official, Li Qianli (李千里), submitted two young eunuchs to Wu Zetian, who had by that point taken the throne as "emperor," as tribute; one was Lishi (who had not yet taken the name of Gao at this point), and one was named Jin'gang (金剛). Wu Zetian favored Lishi for his intelligence and kept him as an attending eunuch. Later, however, Lishi committed a minor fault, and she had him battered and expelled from her presence. An older eunuch, Gao Yanfu (高延福), took Lishi as an adoptive son (and thus had Lishi take his own name of Gao), and as Gao Yanfu had previously served Wu Zetian's powerful nephew Wu Sansi the Prince of Liang, he had Gao Lishi serve Wu Sansi. After about a year, Wu Zetian summoned him back to her palace, and he again attended her. He eventually grew to be exceedingly tall. As he was careful, he was put in charge of announcing imperial edicts, and was eventually promoted to be *Gongwei Cheng* (宮闈丞), a highly ranked eunuch.

During the subsequent return to the throne by Emperor Zhongzong, Gao Lishi cultivated a friendship with Emperor Zhongzong's nephew Li Longji the Prince of Linzi, the son of Li Dan the Prince of Xiang (Emperor Zhongzong's brother and former emperor). In 705, after Emperor Zhongzong's sudden death, Li Longji and Emperor Zhongzong's sister Princess Taiping overthrew Emperor Zhongzong's powerful wife Empress Wei and returned Li Dan to the throne. Li Longji was created crown prince, and he retained Gao on his staff.

During Emperor Xuanzong's reign

In 712, Emperor Ruizong passed the throne to Li Longji, who took the throne as Emperor Xuanzong. However, Emperor Ruizong retained most of the imperial authority as *Taishang Huang* (retired emperor), and Princess Taiping, through him, continued to exert great influence on governance. As of 713, it was said that five of the seven chancellors at the time -- Dou Huaizhen, Cen Xi, Xiao Zhizhong, Cui Shi, and Lu Xiangxian -- were recommended by her (although Lu was not considered a follower of hers). With Emperor Xuanzong and Princess Taiping locked into a power struggle, Zhang Shuo, from his post at Luoyang, had a messenger present Emperor Xuanzong with his sword -- meaning to tell him that it was time to take decisive action. Meanwhile, it was said that Princess Taiping, Dou, Cen, Xiao, and Cui; along with other officials Xue Ji, Li Jin (李晉) the Prince of Xinxing (a grandson of Li Deliang (李德良), a cousin of Tang's founder Emperor Gaozu), Li You (李猷), Jia Yingfu (賈膺福), Tang Jun (唐晙); the generals Chang Yuankai (常元楷), Li Ci (李慈), and Li Qin (李欽); and the monk Huifan (惠範), were plotting to overthrow Emperor Xuanzong. It was further said that they discussed, with the lady in waiting Lady Yuan to poison the *gastrodia elata* that Emperor Xuanzong routinely took as an aphrodisiac. When this alleged plot was reported to Emperor Xuanzong by Wei Zhigu, Emperor Xuanzong, who had already received advice from Wang Ju (王琚), Zhang Shuo, and Cui Riyong to act first, did so. He convened a meeting with his brothers Li Fan (李範) the Prince of Qi, Li Ye (李業) the Prince of Xue, Guo, along with a number of his associates — the general Wang Maozhong (王毛仲), the officials Jiang Jiao (姜皎) and Li Lingwen (李令問), his brother-in-law Wang Shouyi (王守一), Gao Lishi, and the military officer Li Shoude (李守德) — and decided to act first. On July 29, Emperor Xuanzong had Wang Maozhong take 300 soldiers to the imperial guard camp to behead Chang and Li Ci. Then, Jia, Li You, Xiao, and Cen were arrested and executed as well. Dou and Princess Taiping committed suicide. Emperor Ruizong turned over imperial authority to Emperor Xuanzong and thereafter was no longer involved in important decisions. As a result of Gao's participation in this action against Princess Taiping and her party, Emperor Xuanzong awarded him by making him a general of the imperial guards, as well as the acting head of the eunuch bureau (內侍省, *Neishi Sheng*). Gao's general commission made Gao the first eunuch in Tang history to carry the third rank in Tang's nine-rank system, and this was viewed as the start of the rise of eunuchs.

Afterwards Gao became one of Emperor Xuanzong's closest confidants, and it was often Gao that Emperor Xuanzong sent to communicate his wishes with key officials. For example, later in 713, when the chancellor Yao Yuanzhi was initially surprised and dismayed when Emperor Xuanzong refused to discuss the commissions of low-level officials with him, Gao spoke with Emperor Xuanzong and was told that the reason was not that he was displeased with Yao, but rather that these were decisions that Yao himself, as chancellor, had the authority to make. After Gao informed Yao this, Yao's apprehensions were dissolved. In 726, when Zhang Shuo was accused of corruption and arrested, it was Gao that Emperor Xuanzong sent to visit Zhang to see how he was doing, and it was at Gao's subsequent intercession that Zhang's punishment was reduced.

In 730, when Emperor Xuanzong was beginning to be apprehensive about Wang Maozhong's power and arrogance, it was Gao who suggested that he act first, and in spring 731, Emperor Xuanzong exiled Wang and his associates, and subsequently forced Wang to commit suicide. Thereafter it was said that Gao was particularly trusted by Emperor Xuanzong, who remarked, "If Gao Lishi is here, I can sleep securely." Gao therefore rarely returned to his own home, and the petitions submitted to Emperor Xuanzong were first screened by Gao before he would pass them on to Emperor Xuanzong—and Gao ruled on the less important matters himself, causing his power to rise immensely. He spent much effort to support his adoptive parents Gao Yanfu and Gao Yanfu's wife. He also had the commander (*jiedushi*) of Lingnan Circuit locate his birth mother Lady Mai and send her to the capital Chang'an, so that he could support her. When Lady Mai died, the general Cheng Boxian (程伯獻) and the official Feng Shaozheng (馮紹正), who had sworn to be brothers with Gao Lishi, both mourned her deeply. Gao Lishi's father-in-law Lü Xuanwu (呂玄晤) was promoted quickly, as were his brothers and sons, and when Gao Lishi's wife Lady Lü died, the officials and the ordinary citizens all mourned her, to impress Gao. However, it was said that while Gao was powerful, he was careful and modest, and therefore continuously drew trust from Emperor Xuanzong. Among officials and generals who ingratiated him and had him help their advancements were Yuwen Rong, Li Linfu, Li Shizhi, Gai Jiayun (蓋嘉運), Wei Jian (韋堅), Yang Shenjin (楊慎矜), Wang Hong (王鉷), Yang Guozhong, An Lushan, An Sishun, and Gao Xianzhi. The intelligentsia at the time blamed him for the advancement of some of the more power-hungry officials, but also recognized that whenever officials associated with him were charged with crimes, he would not improperly intercede to save them.

In 737, Emperor Xuanzong's favorite concubine Consort Wu, trying to have her son Li Mao (李瑁) the Prince of Shou made crown prince, made false accusations against Li Ying the Crown Prince, as well as two other princes, Li Yao (李瑤) the Prince of E and Li Ju (李琚) the Prince of Guang. Li Ying, Li Yao, and Li Ju were deposed and then forced to commit suicide. Consort Wu died later that year, but Li Linfu, who was then chancellor and who was allied with her, continued to lobby on Li Mao's behalf. Instead, Emperor Xuanzong was considering an older son, Li Yu the Prince of Zhong, but could not decide quickly, and was depressed over the matter as well as his killing of three of his own sons. He could not sleep well or eat well. Gao asked him the reason, and he responded, "You are my old servant. Can you not tell?" Gao responded, "Is it that the position of young master [(i.e., crown prince)] has not been decided?" He responded, "Yes." Gao responded, "You do not need to trouble your heart. Just select the oldest one, and no one would dare to dispute it." Emperor Xuanzong therefore made up his mind, and he selected Li Yu (whose name was later changed to Li Heng) as crown prince.

Meanwhile, it was customary for Tang emperors to rotate their residences between Chang'an and the eastern capital Luoyang, depending on the amount of harvests for the year, as it was easier to transport food supplies to Luoyang than Chang'an. However, after Emperor Xuanzong last returned to Chang'an from Luoyang in 736, he did not visit Luoyang again. Li Linfu knew that he, in his more advanced age (he was 49 as of 736), tired of the rotation, and therefore expended effort to build up food supplies within the Guanzhong region, centered around Chang'an. By 744, on one occasion, Emperor Xuanzong commented to Gao:

It has been almost 10 years since I have left Chang'an. The realm is peaceful, and I want to rest and do nothing, giving governance to Li Linfu. What do you think?

Gao, who did not trust Li Linfu, responded:

Since ancient times, it was customary for the Son of Heaven to visit places throughout the realm. In addition, the powers of governance should not be easily given to others. If his authority is established, who would dare to oppose him?

Emperor Xuanzong was displeased, and Gao bowed and stated, "I am insane. I did not know what I said, and I should be killed." Emperor Xuanzong tried to make light of the situation by holding a feast for Gao, but Gao did not dare to discuss governmental matters with Emperor Xuanzong after this point.

In 746, there was an occasion when Emperor Xuanzong's new favorite concubine, Consort Yang Yuhuan, angered Emperor Xuanzong by being jealous and rude to him, and he had her sent to the mansion of her cousin Yang Xian (楊銛). Later that day, however, his mood was such that he could not eat, and the servants were battered by him for minor offenses. Gao knew that he missed Consort Yang, and Gao requested that the treasures in Consort Yang's palace be sent to her. Emperor Xuanzong agreed, and further sent imperial meals to her as well. That night, Gao requested that Emperor Xuanzong welcome Consort Yang back to the palace, a request that Emperor Xuanzong easily agreed to. Thereafter, she was even more favored, and no other imperial consort drew the favor of Emperor Xuanzong.

Meanwhile, it was said that Li Linfu did not have a good relationship with Li Heng the Crown Prince. Gao often protected Li Heng from the machinations, however, and Li Heng's position was never actually endangered. As a result, Li Heng referred to Gao as an older brother. The other princes and dukes referred to him as "father," and Emperor Xuanzong's sons-in-law referred to him as "master." By 748, he was given the very high general rank of *Piaoqi Da Jiangjun* (驃騎大將軍) and was also carrying the title of Duke of Bohai.

In 750, there was another occasion at which Consort Yang offended Emperor Xuanzong with her words, and he sent her back to her clan. The official Ji Wen (吉溫) told Emperor Xuanzong that he overreacted, and Emperor Xuanzong regretted his actions. He against sent imperial meals to her, and she wept to the eunuchs delivering the meal, stating:

My offense deserves death, and it is fortunate that His Imperial Majesty did not kill me, but instead returned me to my household. I will forever leave the palace. My gold, jade, and treasures were all given me by His Imperial Majesty, and it would be inappropriate for me to offer them back to him. Only what my parents gave me I would dare to offer.

She cut off some of her hair and had the hair taken back to Emperor Xuanzong. Emperor Xuanzong had Gao escort her back to the palace, and thereafter loved her even more.

In 752, when associates of Wang Hong's brother Wang Han (王銲) plotted treason and rose in rebellion inside Chang'an, the troops commanded by Yang Guozhong (Consort Yang's cousin) and Wang Hong were initially unable to crush Wang Han's associates, but Gao then arrived with reinforcements and crushed the rebellion decisively. In the aftermaths, when Wang Hong hesitated at asking for punishment for his brother, Yang Guozhong accused Wang Hong of being complicit, and both Wang Hong and Wang Han were executed. Later that year, when Emperor Xuanzong, seeing that Geshu Han, the commander of Longyou Circuit (隴右, headquartered in modern Haidong Prefecture, Qinghai), had poor relations with An Lushan, then the commander of Fanyang Circuit (范陽, headquartered in modern Beijing) and An Sishun (whose uncle was An Lushan's stepfather), then the commander of Shuofang Circuit (朔方, headquartered in modern Yinchuan, Ningxia), and wanted to improve relations between these three key border troop commanders, he summoned all three to the capital and had Gao host a feast for the three of them, trying to get them to resolve their unpleasantries. However, instead, at the feast, Geshu and An Lushan got into an argument, which only stopped after Gao gazed at Geshu, stopping him from responding to An Lushan's insults.

By 754, Yang Guozhong, who was then chancellor, was beginning to repeatedly accuse An Lushan of plotting rebellion, claiming that if Emperor Xuanzong summoned An to the capital, An would surely not come. Instead, when Emperor Xuanzong summoned An to the capital in early 754, An came. Emperor Xuanzong considered making him chancellor as well—even having the official Zhang Ji (張垍, Zhang Shuo's son) draft an edict to that effect—but eventually did not do so. When An was set to return to Fanyang, Emperor Xuanzong had Gao hold a feast for An to send him off. After the feast, Gao observed to Emperor Xuanzong that An was somewhat displeased, perhaps because he had found out that he was originally set to be made chancellor but was not. Emperor Xuanzong, believing Zhang Ji and his brothers Zhang Jun (張均) and Zhang Shu (張埱) to have leaked the news, demoted all of them. Meanwhile, there was a war in the southwest between Tang forces and Nanzhao, which was not going well for Tang, and 200,000 soldiers had died in the conflict. Yang Guozhong, however, was hiding the truth from Emperor Xuanzong and declaring that there had been numerous victories. In response, Emperor Xuanzong told Gao:
I am old now. I entrust the governmental matters to the chancellors, and the border matters to the generals. I do not worry about them.
Gao responded, however, as he saw trouble brewing:
I heard that we were suffering repeated losses in Yunnan, and the border generals are wielding too much power. How can Your Imperial Majesty control the situation? If a rebellion erupts, there is no way to stop it. How can you have no worries?
Emperor Xuanzong began to be concerned, but took no decisive action, instead stating, "Do not speak further. Let me think about these things."

At the time, Yang Guozhong was also hiding a major flood from Emperor Xuanzong. Once, when Emperor Xuanzong was alone with Gao, he stated, "The rains would not stop. Speak what you will." Gao responded, "Since Your Imperial Majesty trusted all power to the chancellors, the rewards and punishments are out of hand, and the yin and yang are out of alignment. How would I dare to speak?"

Meanwhile, Yang Guozhong repeatedly tried to provoke An into rebelling, including arresting and executing staff members at An's mansion in Chang'an. In 755, An finally did. In 756, after Geshu was defeated by An's forces, after being forced by Yang Guozhong to engage An, Tong Pass, the last major defense against An's forces, fell to An. Yang Guozhong suggested fleeing to Chengdu, the capital of Jiannan Circuit, of which Yang Guozhong was commander. On July 14, Emperor Xuanzong, keeping the news secret from the people of Chang'an, took the imperial guards to escort him, Consort Yang, her family, and his immediate clan members, and exited Chang'an, heading toward Chengdu. Attending him were Yang Guozhong, his fellow chancellor Wei Jiansu, the official Wei Fangjin (魏方進), the general Chen Xuanli (陳玄禮), and some eunuchs and ladies in waiting close to him, including Gao.

On July 15, Emperor Xuanzong's train reached Mawei Station (馬嵬驛, in modern Xianyang, Shaanxi). The imperial guards were not fed and were angry at Yang Guozhong. Chen also believed that Yang Guozhong provoked this disaster and planned to carry him—and reported his plans to Li Heng through Li Heng's eunuch Li Fuguo, but Li Heng was hesitated and gave no approval. Meanwhile, though, Tufan emissaries, who followed Emperor Xuanzong south, were meeting with Yang Guozhong and complaining that they were also not fed. The imperial guard soldiers took this opportunity to proclaim that Yang Guozhong was planning treason along with the Tufan emissaries, and they killed him, along with his son Yang Xuan (楊暄), the Ladies of Han and Qin, and Wei Fangjin. Wei Jiansu was also nearly killed, but was spared at the last moment with severe injuries. The soldiers then surrounded Emperor Xuanzong's pavilion, and refused to scatter even after Emperor Xuanzong came out to comfort them and order them to scatter. Chen publicly urged him to put Consort Yang to death—which Emperor Xuanzong initially declined. After Wei Jiansu's son Wei E (韋諤) and Gao Lishi spoke further, Emperor Xuanzong finally resolved to do so. He therefore had Gao take Consort Yang to a Buddhist shrine and strangle her there. After he showed the body to Chen and the other imperial guard generals, the guard soldiers finally scattered and prepared for further movement. The imperial guards eventually escorted Emperor Xuanzong to Chengdu. Gao continued to attend to him there. For Gao's faithfulness, Emperor Xuanzong created him the Duke of Qi.

During Emperor Suzong's reign
Li Heng, however, broke away from Emperor Xuanzong's party and fled to Shuofang instead, and was proclaimed emperor there (as Emperor Suzong) later in 756, a proclamation that Emperor Xuanzong recognized, as he assumed the title of *Taishang Huang* and had only relatively limited authority thereafter.

In 757, after Emperor Suzong recaptured Chang'an, he welcomed Emperor Xuanzong back to Chang'an. Gao Lishi accompanied Emperor Xuanzong back to the capital, and was rewarded with the honorific title *Kaifu Yitong Sansi* (開府儀同三司).

After Emperor Xuanzong's return to Chang'an, he took residence at Xingqing Palace (興慶宮), which was converted from his residence as an imperial prince. Gao and Chen Xuanli attended to him, as did Emperor Xuanzong's younger sister Li Chiying (李持盈) the Princess Yuzhen, the lady in waiting Ru Xianyuan (如仙媛), and the eunuchs Wang Cheng'en (王承恩) and Wei Yue (魏悅). Meanwhile, Li Fuguo had become very powerful, but these attendants of Emperor Xuanzong did not respect him. To retaliate, Li Fuguo began to try to convince Emperor Suzong that Emperor Xuanzong and his attendants were plotting to seize power back. In 760, with Emperor Suzong's tacit, although not explicit, approval, on one occasion when Emperor Xuanzong was out riding, Li Fuguo intercepted him and forced him to move back to the main palace. Even on that occasion, however, Gao would not submit to Li Fuguo, and even yelled at Li Fuguo to force him to get off his horse and to escort Emperor Xuanzong on foot, along with Gao. Soon after Emperor Xuanzong was forcibly moved, Li Fuguo forced Chen to retire, Li Chiying to return to her temple (she had become an ordained Taoist nun in 711), and exiled Gao, Wang, Wei, and Ru. In Gao's case, he was exiled to Wu Prefecture (巫州, roughly modern Huaihua, Hunan).

Death

In spring 762, Emperor Suzong, then seriously ill, declared a general pardon. Gao Lishi was therefore allowed to return to Chang'an, and he began to undertake the journey. While he was on the way back to Chang'an, however, on May 5, Emperor Xuanzong died, followed by Emperor Suzong on May 16. When Gao reached Lang Prefecture (朗州, roughly modern Changde, Hunan), he heard of the two emperors' deaths, and he, mourning Emperor Xuanzong bitterly, spit up blood and died soon afterwards.

Emperor Suzong's son Emperor Daizong, who became emperor after Emperor Suzong's death, recognizing Gao's faithfulness and prior protection of Emperor Suzong, posthumously restored his titles and further bestowed honors, and buried him near Emperor Xuanzong's tomb.

Source (edited): "http://en.wikipedia.org/wiki/Gao_Lishi"

Li Fuguo

Li Fuguo (李輔國; 704 – November 8, 762), né **Li Jingzhong** (李靜忠), known from 757 to 758 as **Li Huguo** (李護國), formally **Prince Chou of Bolu** (博陸醜王), was a eunuch official during the reign of Emperor Suzong (Li Heng) of the Chinese dynasty Tang Dynasty. He had served Li Heng while Li Heng was crown prince under Li Heng's father Emperor Xuanzong and later supported Li Heng in ascending the throne during Anshi Rebellion, when Emperor Xuanzong's realm was thrown into confusion. He later became exceedingly powerful, in alliance with Emperor Suzong's wife Empress Zhang, but broke with her and killed her in 762 when Emperor Suzong died. He briefly became the paramount figure in the administration of Emperor Suzong's son and successor Emperor Daizong, but was removed and then killed by assassins sent by Emperor Daizong later that year.

Background

Li Jingzhong was born in 704, during the reign of Wu Zetian. He was castrated early in his childhood, and became a servant at the imperial stables. He was said to be ugly in appearance, but knew how to read and write, and eventually became a servant of the powerful eunuch Gao Lishi. When he was in his 40s, he became in charge of the imperial stables' financial accounts. During the *Tianbao* era (742–756) of Wu Zetian's grandson Emperor Xuanzong, the official Wang Hong (王鉷), who oversaw the imperial stables, was impressed with Li Jingzhong's management of the stables and recommended him to serve on the staff of Emperor Xuanzong's crown prince Li Heng. He soon became a trusted servant of Li Heng's.

In 755, the general An Lushan rebelled against Emperor Xuanzong's rule, and by 756 was approaching the Tang Dynasty capital Chang'an, forcing Emperor Xuanzong and Li Heng to flee. During flight, the angry imperial guard soldiers escorting them killed the chancellor Yang Guozhong and his cousin (Emperor Xuanzong's favorite concubine) Consort Yang Yuhuan, whom they blamed for An's rebellion. After Yang Guozhong's and Consort Yang's deaths, Emperor Xuanzong was intent to continue to head to Jiannan Circuit (劍南, modern Sichuan and Chongqing), but Li Heng, at the suggestion of his son Li Tan the Prince of Jianning and Li Fuguo, decided to take some of the soldiers and head for the important border defense post Lingwu, and Li Jingzhong subsequently accompanied Li Heng to Lingwu, where Li Heng was declared emperor (as Emperor Suzong).

During Emperor Suzong's reign

After Emperor Suzong took the throne, while he did not at that point make his oldest son Li Chu the Prince of Guangping crown prince, he gave Li Chu the title of supreme commander of the armies, and he gave Li Jingzhong dual titles on Li Chu's staff—serving as the head of the crown prince's household (太子家令, *Taizi Jialing*) (although Li Chu was not yet crown prince) and acting assistant of military affairs to the supreme commander (元帥府行軍司馬, *Yuanshuai Fu Xingjun Sima*). Emperor Suzong entrusted Li Jingzhong with the important secrets, and Li Fuguo became in charge of receiving important reports, as well as distributing military command seals and signs. He also changed Li Jingzhong's name to Huguo (meaning, "one who protects the state"). By this point, Li Huguo ate a vegetarian diet and often acted as Buddhist monks did; further, when he was taking a break, he would often hold prayer beads, and people believed at that point he was benevolent. Later, when Emperor Suzong, while still fighting Yan forces, moved his headquarters from Lingwu to Fengxiang (鳳翔, in modern Baoji, Shaanxi) in spring 757, he gave Li Huguo a slightly greater title as the head of the crown prince's household (太子詹事, Taizi Zhanshi), and changed his name again to Fuguo (meaning, "one who assists the state").

During this time, Li Fuguo had been allied with Emperor Suzong's favorite concubine Consort Zhang, and they had a rivalry with Li Tan and Emperor Suzong's trusted advisor Li Mi. Li Tan often accused Li Fuguo and Consort Zhang of improprieties, and further, despite Li Mi's advice to the contrary, plotted to kill them. Li Fuguo and Consort Zhang, instead, acted first, accusing Li Tan of plotting to kill Li Chu. Emperor Suzong, in anger, ordered Li Tan to commit suicide. Li Chu, in fear, also plotted to kill Li Fuguo and Consort Zhang, although, at Li Mi's urging, stopped the plans.

After joint Tang and Huige forces recaptured Chang'an later in 757 under Li Chu's command, Emperor Suzong returned to Chang'an. He bestowed on Li Fuguo a number of titles that gave him responsibility over a number of financial affairs of the state. He also gave Li Fuguo the honorific title of *Kaifu Yitong Sansi* (開府儀同三司) and created him the Duke of Cheng. The officials' reports continued to go through Li Fuguo, and Li Fuguo established a bureau with a number of agents with the responsibility of secretly finding out officials' faults. Even criminal cases were ruled on by Li Fuguo, and he was often making orders, in Emperor Suzong's name, reversing officials' decisions. No official dared to speak against him or even to refer to him by official title, instead addressing him as "Master Five," using a form of address from a servant to a master. (This implied that Li Fuguo was probably a fifth-born son.) Even the chancellor Li Kui, who was from a highly honored household, paid him respect as a son or a nephew would, calling him, "Father Five." Emperor Suzong also gave Li Fuguo, despite his eunuch status, the grandnephew of the deceased official Yuan Xisheng (元希聲) as his wife, and promoted Lady Yuan's uncle.

In 759, after Li Xian became chancellor, he secretly and earnestly pointed out to Emperor Suzong the evils that Li Fuguo's secret agents were carrying out, and Emperor Suzong, in response, issued an edict that, while confirming Li Fuguo's past acts as authorized by imperial authority, ordered that in the future, criminal cases were to be decided and appealed through official channels, thus depriving Li Fuguo of a source of power and causing him to be resentful of Li Xian. Later in the year, after Li Xian and Li Fuguo had an open conflict over the criminal charges against an imperial stable official that led to that official's execution, Li Fuguo convinced Emperor Suzong that Li Xian was simply grabbing power, and Emperor Suzong exiled Li Xian.

After Emperor Xuanzong's return to Chang'an, he took residence at Xingqing Palace (興慶宮), which was converted from his residence as an imperial prince. Gao Lishi and the general Chen Xuanli (陳玄禮) attended to him, as did Emperor Xuanzong's younger sister Li Chiying (李持盈) the Princess Yuzhen, the lady in waiting Ru Xianyuan (如仙媛), and the eunuchs Wang Cheng'en (王承恩) and Wei Yue (魏悅). These attendants of Emperor Xuanzong did not respect Li Fuguo. To retaliate, Li Fuguo began to try to convince Emperor Suzong that Emperor Xuanzong and his attendants were plotting to seize power back. In 760, with Emperor Suzong's tacit, although not explicit, approval, on one occasion when Emperor Xuanzong was out riding, Li Fuguo intercepted him and forced him to move back to the main palace. Even on that occasion, however, Gao would not submit to Li Fuguo, and even yelled at Li Fuguo to force him to get off his horse and to escort Emperor Xuanzong on foot, along with Gao. Soon after Emperor Xuanzong was forcibly moved, Li Fuguo forced Chen to retire, Li Chiying to return to her temple (she had become an ordained Taoist nun in 711), and exiled Gao, Wang, Wei, and Ru. Emperor Suzong had his daughters Princesses Wan'an and Xianyi attend to Emperor Xuanzong, but Emperor Xuanzong, depressed over his forced movement and the exile of his attendants, began to be ill. Emperor Suzong regretted this and considered killing Li Fuguo, but feared the fact that Li Fuguo had command of the imperial guards, and therefore did not act.

In 761, Li Fuguo was made the minister of defense (兵部尚書, *Bingbu Shangshu*), but further wanted to be chancellor. Emperor Suzong, who by this point was fearful of Li Fuguo, refused on the basis that he did not have the support of the officials, Li Fuguo tried to persuade Pei Mian, a senior official who had previously been chancellor, to recommend him. Emperor Suzong told the chancellor Xiao Hua that if an important official (i.e., someone like Pei) recommended Li Fuguo, he would no longer have the excuse to refuse Li Fuguo's request. When Xiao subsequently discussed this with Pei, Pei adamantly stated that he would never allow Li Fuguo to be chancellor. Subsequently, Li Fuguo was not able to be chancellor while Emperor Suzong was alive, much to Li Fuguo's resentment. In 762, bearing a grudge against Xiao, he insisted to Emperor Suzong that Xiao be removed and replaced with Yuan Zai.

Throughout the years, Empress Zhang and Li Fuguo's alliance held. However, as of spring 762, when both Emperors Xuanzong and Suzong were seriously ill, Empress Zhang and Li Fuguo had begun to be rivals. She summoned Li Chu (whose name had been changed to Li Yu and who had been created crown prince) and tried to persuade him to join her in killing Li Fuguo and his ally Cheng Yuanzhen. Li Yu declined, and she instead tried to persuade his younger brother Li Xi (李係) the Prince of Yue, to join her. Li Xi agreed. She and Li Xi thereafter had the eunuch Duan Hengjun (段恆俊) selected some 200 strong eunuchs, ready to ambush Li Fuguo and Cheng. On May 14, Empress Zhang issued an order in Emperor Suzong's name, summoning Li Yu. Cheng found out and informed Li

Fuguo, who intercepted Li Yu at the palace gate and then escorted him to the camp of the imperial guards under Li Fuguo's command. The guards under Li Fuguo's command then entered the palace and arrested Empress Zhang and Li Xi; the other eunuchs and ladies in waiting fled, leaving Emperor Suzong without care. On May 16, Emperor Suzong died, and Li Fuguo thereafter executed Empress Zhang and Li Xi, as well as Li Xian the Prince of Yan, and then declared Li Yu emperor (as Emperor Daizong).

During Emperor Daizong's reign

After Emperor Daizong took the throne, Li Fuguo became even more arrogant, stating to him,

You, Emperor, just remain in the palace. Let this old servant of yours handle what is outside.

Emperor Daizong was secretly displeased, but in order to placate Li Fuguo, gave him the title of *Shangfu* (尚父, meaning, "like father") and ordered that he not be referred to by name. He also made Li Fuguo *Sikong* (司空, one of the Three Excellencies) and *Zhongshu Ling* (中書令) -- the head of the legislative bureau of government (中書省, *Zhongshu Sheng*) and a post considered one for a chancellor. Li Fuguo gave a major part of the command responsibilities to Cheng Yuanzhen. Carrying out further retaliation against Xiao Hua, Li Fuguo had Xiao further demoted.

Meanwhile, though, Li Fuguo did not expect that both Emperor Daizong and Cheng, who wanted more power, would turn against him. In summer 762, at Cheng's secret suggestion, Emperor Daizong issued an edict that stripped Li Fuguo of the titles of minister of defense and assistant of military affairs to the supreme commander—thus stripping him of military command—giving the latter post to Cheng. He also ordered Li Fuguo to leave the palace and take residence up outside, although he created Li Fuguo the Prince of Bolu. Li Fuguo became apprehensive and offered to retire, and Emperor Daizong declined and sent him away with formal respect.

Because Li Fuguo had killed Empress Zhang and had supported him for the throne, Emperor Daizong did not want to kill him openly. Instead, on November 8, 762, an assassin got into Li Fuguo's mansion and killed him, taking his head and an arm away as well. Emperor Daizong formally issued an order seeking the arrest of the assassin, and buried Li Fuguo in a grand ceremony, after having a wooden head and wooden arm carved to be buried with the rest of the body, although he gave Li Fuguo the unflattering posthumous name of Chou (醜, meaning "power abuser").

Source (edited): "http://en.wikipedia.org/wiki/Li_Fuguo"

Qiu Shiliang

Qiu Shiliang (仇士良) (died 843), courtesy name **Kuangmei** (匡美), formally the **Duke of Chu** (楚公), was an eunuch official of the Chinese dynasty Tang Dynasty, becoming particularly powerful after the Ganlu Incident — an event in which Emperor Wenzong tried, but failed, to seize power back from powerful eunuchs by slaughtering them.

Background and early career

It is not known when Qiu Shiliang was born, but it was known that he was from Xun Prefecture (循州, in modern Huizhou, Guangdong). During the brief reign of Emperor Shunzong (805), Qiu became a servant to Emperor Shunzong's crown prince Li Chun, and after Li Chun became emperor later that year (as Emperor Xianzong), he became an imperial attendant, and later served as the eunuch monitor of the army to such circuits as Pinglu (平盧, headquartered in modern Weifang, Shandong) and Fengxiang (鳳翔, headquartered in modern Baoji, Shaanxi). On an occasion, when both he and the imperial censor Yuan Zhen happened to be at the imperial messenger outpost Fushui (敷水, in modern Weinan, Shaanxi), he and Yuan got into a dispute over who had the right to use the main bedroom at the outpost, and he battered and injured Yuan. After the incident, Yuan's superior, the deputy chief imperial censor Wang Bo proposed that the matter be handled per the previous formal policy that whenever an imperial censor and an imperial messenger arrived at the same location, the one who arrived first should have precedence. Emperor Xianzong, favoring Qiu, demoted Yuan, rather than to look further into the matter. Through the rest of Emperor Xianzong's reign and the reigns of his son Emperor Muzong and grandson Emperor Jingzong, Qiu often served as the director of the imperial servants (五坊使, *Wufangshi*), and it was said that he was harsh to the people, often allowing his subordinates to pillage them.

Around new year 827, Emperor Jingzong was assassinated by a group of eunuchs and officers resentful of his harsh temperament. The conspirators initially tried to make Emperor Muzong's brother Li Wu the Prince of Jiàng emperor, but another group of eunuchs — led by the directors of palace communications Wang Shoucheng and Yang Chenghe (楊承和) and the commanders of the Shence Armies Wei Congjian (魏從簡) and Liang Shouqian (梁守謙), and Qiu, who was then a general of the Shence Army as well, was a part of this group — attacked the conspirators, killing them and Li Wu. This group of eunuchs made Emperor Jingzong's younger brother Li Han the Prince of Jiāng (note different tone) emperor (as Emperor Wenzong). Despite Qiu's participation in the counterattack, however, because Wang suppressed Qiu, Qiu was not rewarded, and from this point on he resented Wang.

During Emperor Wenzong's reign

Before the Ganlu Incident

As of 835, Emperor Wenzong was conspiring with the officials Zheng Zhu and Li Xun to slaughter the powerful eunuchs. They first wanted to target Wang Shoucheng, and as they knew that Wang and Qiu Shiliang were enemies, in summer 835 Emperor Wenzong made Qiu the commander of the Left Shence Army so that he would divert Wang's authority. Subsequently, after Wang retired, Emperor Wenzong had the eunuch Li Haogu (李好古) send poisoned wine to Wang, and Wang died shortly thereafter.

The Ganlu Incident

Wang Shoucheng's death, however, was only a small part of Emperor Wenzong's planning with Zheng Zhu and Li Xun — they planned to use the occasion of Wang's funeral to gather the eunuchs, and then have Zheng's troops (as Zheng was then the military governor (*Jiedushi*) of Fengxiang Circuit (鳳翔), headquartered in modern Baoji, Shaanxi)) slaughter them. (Unknown to Zheng and Emperor Wenzong, Li Xun had, by this point, grown jealous of Zheng as well, and so was instead gathering troops commanded by his associates Guo Xingyu (郭行餘), Wang Fan (王璠), Luo Liyan (羅立言), Han Yue (韓約), and Li Xiaoben (李孝本) to carry out the slaughter; he planned to, after the slaughter, kill Zheng as well.

On December 14, 835, six days before the scheduled funeral for Wang, Han reported to Emperor Wenzong, at the imperial meeting hall Zichen Hall (紫宸殿), that there had been sweet dew (甘露, *ganlu* in Chinese) that appeared on a pomegranate tree outside the headquarters of Zuo Jinwu (左金吾), one of the Wei Army (衛軍) headquarters — viewed as a sign of divine favor. Emperor Wenzong then went to nearby Hanyuan Hall (含元殿) and ordered the imperial officials, including Li Xun, to examine the purported sweet dew. Li Xun soon returned and stated that it appeared that there was no sweet dew; at Li Xun's suggestion, Emperor Wenzong ordered Qiu and his fellow Shence Army commander Yu Hongzhi (魚弘志) to lead the eunuchs in examining the sweet dew. When Qiu and Yu arrived at the Zuo Jinwu headquarters, however, Han had lost his composure, and Qiu realized that something was wrong when he saw soldiers converging and the noise of weapons clanging. He and the other eunuchs immediately ran back to Hanyuan Hall and seized Emperor Wenzong. The soldiers under Luo and Li Xiaoben battled the eunuchs, killing a number of them, but the eunuchs were able to escort Emperor Wenzong back to the imperial palace. Knowing that he had lost this gambit, Li Xun fled.

Once the eunuchs took Emperor Wenzong back to the palace, they realized that Emperor Wenzong was complicit in this plot to slaughter them, and they cursed him and held him. Qiu then ordered the Shence Army officers Liu Tailun (劉泰倫) and Wei Zhongqing (魏仲卿) to search and arrest Li Xun. The Shence Army soldiers took this chance to slaughter many imperial officials and Wei Army soldiers,. Eventually, Li Xun and his conspirators were found and executed, along with the chancellors Wang Ya, Jia Su, and Shu Yuanyu, who were not involved in the plot but whom Qiu and the other eunuchs held responsible as well. At Qiu's order, Zheng was killed by the eunuch monitor of Fengxiang, Zhang Zhongqing (張仲卿). From this point on, Qiu was the leading figure at the imperial court, with even Emperor Wenzong under the eunuchs' control. Qiu was given an honorary general title as well as the honorific title of *Tejin* (特進).

After the Ganlu Incident

From thereon, few officials dared to stand up to Qiu Shiliang, although late in 835, there was an incident in which Xue Yuanshang (薛元賞) the mayor of Jingzhao Municipality (京兆, i.e., the region of the capital Chang'an) executed a Shence Army officer who was being disrespectful to the chancellor Li Shi, and then met Qiu to apologize. Qiu, knowing that the officer could not be brought back to life, feasted with Xue. In 836, Qiu suggested that Shence Army soldiers guard the palace, instead of the Jinwu Corps (i.e., Zuo Jinwu and You Jinwu), but at the opposition of the advisory official Feng Ding (馮定), Qiu's suggestion was not carried out. At one point, Qiu and Yu Hongzhi were so resentful of Emperor Wenzong that they considered deposing him. They summoned the imperial scholar Cui Shenyou (崔慎由) and asked him to draft an edict in the name of Emperor Wenzong's grandmother Grand Empress Dowager Guo deposing Emperor Wenzong on excuses of his being too ill to govern. Cui resisted, pointing out that it would be inappropriate and that he was willing to risk his own life, but not those of his household of 300 people (i.e., if he committed treason, his household would be slaughtered). Qiu and Yu then led Cui to Emperor Wenzong and, in Cui's presence, made various accusations against Emperor Wenzong, and Emperor Wenzong did not dare to respond. Qiu then stated, "If it were not for the imperial scholar, you would not be allowed to remain on this throne." At Qiu's order, Cui kept this matter secret, but wrote secret records of this incident and left them for his son Cui Yin. (It was said that it was because of this incident that Cui Yin, who would later become chancellor under Emperor Zhaozong, was determined to exterminate eunuchs.)

In spring 836, at the suggestion of the senior official Linghu Chu, Emperor Wenzong ordered that Wang Ya and the other executed officials, whose bodies had been exposed to the elements, be properly buried. Qiu, however, secretly sent soldiers to dig up their bodies and throw the bodies into the Wei River.

Meanwhile, Qiu continued to be largely the power controlling the policies at this point. However, after Liu Congjian the military governor of Zhaoyi Circuit (昭義, headquartered in modern Changzhi, Shanxi) submitted several petitions that, in harsh language, defended Wang and accused Qiu and other eunuchs of crimes, Qiu and the other eunuchs began to be apprehensive, and allowed Emperor Wenzong and the chancellors Li Shi and Zheng Tan more room to govern. Soon thereafter, however, there was an incident when there were rumors that Emperor Wenzong was prepared to give the chancellors commands of the armies to again act against the eunuchs, and tensions rose again. It was only after Li Shi proposed that Emperor Wenzong convene a meeting between the chancellors and the eunuchs, allowing Li Shi and Zheng to explain what was happening to the eunuchs, that Qiu and the others were less suspicious of the chancellors.

Meanwhile, Qiu had been resentful of the military governor of Fufang Circuit (鄜坊, headquartered in modern Yan'an, Shaanxi), Xiao Hong (蕭洪) — who was not a real brother of Emperor Wenzong's mother Empress Dowager Xiao but pretended to be and therefore received official commissions — because Xiao had ingratiated Li Xun and, under Li Xun's protection, had refused to pay bribes that his predecessor had promised to pay the officers of the Shence Armies. Qiu found out that Xiao was not really Empress Dowager Xiao's brother and exposed his deceit; Xiao was exiled and, on the way, ordered to commit suicide.

As Li Shi had been willing to stand up to the eunuchs on policy issues, Qiu began to resent him deeply. In 838, Qiu sent assassins to try to kill Li Shi, but the assassination failed. Despite the failure, Li Shi became fearful and offered to resign his chancellor position. Emperor Wenzong reluctantly agreed, making Li Shi the military governor of Jingnan Circuit (荊南, headquartered in modern Jingzhou, Hubei) instead.

Meanwhile, as Emperor Wenzong's son and crown prince Li Yong died in 838, a question arose as to who would succeed Emperor Wenzong. Emperor Wenzong's favorite concubine Consort Yang supported Emperor Wenzong's younger brother Li Rong the Prince of An, but after opposition by the chancellor Li Jue, Emperor Wenzong created Emperor Jingzong's son Li Chengmei the Prince of Chen crown prince. When Emperor Wenzong became deathly ill in spring 840, he had his trusted eunuchs Liu Hongyi (劉弘逸) and Xue Jileng (薛季稜) summon the chancellors Li Jue and Yang Sifu to the palace, preparing to entrust Li Chengmei to them. Qiu and Yu, however, opposed Li Chengmei, as Emperor Wenzong did not consult them before making Li Chengmei crown prince. They discussed with Li Jue and Yang the possibility of changing the crown prince and, despite Li Jue's opposition, issued an edict in Emperor Wenzong's name deposing Li Chengmei and creating Emperor Wenzong's younger brother Li Chan the Prince of Ying crown prince instead. Soon thereafter, Emperor Wenzong died. At Qiu's urging, Li Chan, even before he would officially take the throne, ordered Consort Yang, Li Rong, and Li Chengmei to commit suicide. It was said that this point, Qiu and the other powerful eunuchs resented Emperor Wenzong so much that any eunuchs and musicians whom Emperor Wenzong favored were being executed and exiled en masse. Soon, Li Chan formally took the throne (as Emperor Wuzong).

During Emperor Wuzong's reign

Qiu Shiliang continued to be powerful, initially, in Emperor Wuzong's administration. Emperor Wuzong created him the Duke of Chu. In 840, there was an incident in which Qiu requested that, per Tang regulations that high-level officials be allowed to recommend their sons for official service, his adopted son become an officer for the imperial guards. The imperial attendant Li Zhongmin (李中敏) opposed the request, stating, in provocative language, "Of course, *Kaifu* [(one of the honorific titles that Qiu held)] qualified one to recommend one's son, but how can an eunuch have a son?" Qiu was insulted and angered, and the new chancellor Li Deyu, who resented Yang Sifu (whom Emperor Wuzong had exiled by this point), believed that Li Zhongmin was an associate of Yang's, and therefore had Li Zhongmin exiled.

Meanwhile, Qiu resented Liu Hongyi and Xue Jileng for their close association with Emperor Wenzong. Qiu therefore repeatedly made accusations against them, as well as Yang and Li Jue. In 841 Emperor Wuzong ordered Liu and Xue to commit suicide and, initially, was set to send eunuchs to Tan Prefecture (潭州, in modern Changsha, Hunan, where Yang was then serving as governor of Hunan Circuit (湖南)) and Gui Prefecture (桂州, in modern Guilin, Guangxi, where Li Jue was then serving as the governor of Gui District (桂管)), to order Yang and Li Jue to commit suicide as well. At the intercession of Li Deyu and his fellow chancellors Cui Gong, Cui Dan, and Chen Yixing, Yang and Li Jue were spared their lives, but were further demoted and exiled.

In fall 841, Qiu was given the additional title of the monitor of the Shence Armies (觀軍容使, *Guanjunrongshi*). However, he began to resent Li Deyu for Li Deyu's hold on power as well. In 842, when Emperor Wuzong was planning to issue a general pardon, rumors got to Qiu that, as part of the edict, the chancellors and the director of finances were planning to reduce Shence Army's clothing and food stipends, Qiu publicly declared, "If this occurred, when the pardon is declared, the soldiers will gather in front of Danfeng Tower [(丹鳳樓, the tower from which emperors declared pardons)] and demonstrate!" Emperor Wuzong, angered by the remarks, sent eunuchs to rebuke Qiu and the other Shence Army officers for spreading rumors, and Qiu apologized.

Throughout the years, Qiu and Liu Congjian continued to have an adversarial relationship, as Liu repeatedly accused Qiu of crimes, and Qiu repeatedly accused Liu of plotting to rebel against the imperial government. On one occasion, Liu offered Emperor Wuzong a large horse as a tribute, but Emperor Wuzong did not accept it and returned it to Liu. Liu believed that Emperor Wuzong rejected the horse at Qiu's suggestion and, in anger, killed the horse. Thereafter, Liu acted effectively independently from the imperial government. In 843, when Liu fell ill, he wanted to have his adopted son Liu Zhen (the biological son of his brother Liu

Congsu (劉從素) and therefore his biological nephew) inherit Zhaoyi Circuit. When Emperor Wuzong subsequently refused the request after Liu Congjian's death and instead ordered Liu Zhen to escort Liu Congjian's casket to the eastern capital Luoyang, Liu Zhen resisted, citing the adversarial relationship between Liu Congjian and Qiu as the reason why he did not dare to leave Zhaoyi Circuit. Emperor Wuzong thus declared a campaign against Liu Zhen. (Eventually, the imperial government would prevail in 845, after Qiu himself had died.)

Meanwhile, although Emperor Wuzong outwardly honored Qiu, he actually was suspicious of and despised Qiu. Realizing this, Qiu claimed to be ill and requested to be given less important offices. Emperor Wuzong agreed. Qiu then retired in summer 843. It was said that when he was retiring, the other eunuchs escorted him back to his mansion, and he advised them:

Do not let the Son of Heaven be without something to do. Keep him occupied with a life of luxury and pleasures, with enjoyment for his eyes and ears. We further need to find new methods to keep him freshened, so that he would not have time to do other things. This would be the only way for our will to be done. No matter what, do not let him study or be close to the scholars. If he studied histories of past dynasties, he will be concerned, and he will not be close to us.

The other eunuchs thanked him and bowed to him before leaving.

Qiu died later that year. In 844, however, other eunuchs reported to Emperor Wuzong of Qiu's crimes. Emperor Wuzong had Qiu's mansion searched, and several thousand sets of armors were found. Emperor Wuzong had Qiu posthumously stripped of his titles, and his assets were confiscated.

Source (edited): "http://en.wikipedia.org/wiki/Qiu_Shiliang"

Tian Lingzi

Tian Lingzi (田令孜) (died 893), courtesy name **Zhongze** (仲則), formally the **Duke of Jin** (晉公), was a powerful eunuch during the reign of Emperor Xizong of Tang. During most of Emperor Xizong's reign, he had a stranglehold on power due to his close personal relationship with Emperor Xizong as well as his control over the eunuch-commanded Shence Armies, even throughout Emperor Xizong's flight to Xichuan Circuit (西川, headquartered in modern Chengdu, Sichuan) in the face of Huang Chao's agrarian rebellion. Late in Emperor Xizong's reign, he was forced to give up his powerful position after his dispute with the warlord Wang Chongrong led to multiple rebellions that rendered the Tang court virtually powerless over the warlords, and he was given refuge by his brother Chen Jingxuan, the military governor of Xichuan. In 891, however, Chen was defeated by Wang Jian and forced to surrender Xichuan to Wang. In 893, Wang put Chen and Tian to death.

Background

It is not known when Tian Lingzi was born. He was originally surnamed Chen and had at least two brothers, Chen Jingxuan and Chen Jingxun (陳敬珣). The historical accounts were inconsistent as to whether he was from the Shu (蜀, i.e., modern Sichuan) region (as per his biography in the *New Book of Tang*) or from Xu Prefecture (許州, in modern Xuchang, Henan) (as per the *Zizhi Tongjian* when describing Chen Jingxuan's origins) It was said that he entered the palace as an eunuch under his adoptive father, presumably a eunuch named Tian, during the middle of Emperor Yizong's *Xiantong* era (860-874). It was said that he was literate, read much, and was capable of strategies. During Emperor Yizong's reign, he served as a eunuch who oversaw the imperial stables, and he became close to Emperor Yizong's son Li Yan the Prince of Pu.

During Emperor Xizong's reign

Before Huang Chao's attack on Chang'an

Emperor Yizong died in 873, and Li Yan, with the support of the eunuchs Liu Xingshen (劉行深) and Han Wenyue (韓文約), who were then the commanders of the Shence Armies, was made emperor (as Emperor Xizong). Soon after Emperor Xizong became emperor, he made Tian Lingzi one of the directors of palace communications (樞密使, *Shumishi*), and in 875 further made Tian the commander of the Right Shence Army. It was said that because Emperor Xizong, who was then 13, liked to spend his time in games, he entrusted the matters of state to Tian, and went as far as referring to Tian as "Father." Whenever Tian met with Emperor Xizong, he would prepare two plates of snacks, and they would drink and snack together. At Tian's suggestion, much of the wealth of the Chang'an merchants were seized and placed in the palace storage. Anyone who dared to complain was battered to death, and the imperial officials did not dare to intercede.

As of 880, the Tang realm was being overrun by agrarian rebels, the strongest of which was Huang Chao. As the imperial armies were having difficulty containing the rebellions, Tian began considering the contingency plan, in case Chang'an were attacked, of taking the emperor to the Shu region. He thus recommended his brother Chen Jingxuan, who was then a general of the imperial guards, as well as several generals he trusted, Yang Shili, Niu Xu (牛勗), and Luo Yuangao (羅元杲), as potential military governors for the region, also known as the Sanchuan (三川) — i.e., the three circuits of Xichuan, Dongchuan (東川, headquartered in modern Mianyang, Sichuan), and Shannan West (山南西道, headquartered in modern Hanzhong, Shaanxi). Emperor Xizong had the four of them play a ballgame to determine the order they would be commissioned. Chen won the game, and was made the military governor of Xichuan, while Yang was given Dongchuan and Niu Shannan West. During this period, Tian governed in association with the chancellor Lu Xi.

By winter 880, Huang was approaching Tong Pass. Tian and the chancellor Cui Hang suggested that Emperor Xizong carry out the contingency plan to flee to the Sanchuan region. Emperor Xizong initially refused and ordered Tian to have the imperial guards try to defend Tong Pass. The soldiers that Tian was able to gather, however, were new and inexperienced, and they were unable to aid the imperial forces already gathered at Tong Pass in time. Tian blamed Lu for the defeats, and Lu committed suicide. He then took Emperor Xizong, along with four imperial princes and a few imperial consorts, and fled Chang'an, heading toward Xichuan's capital Chengdu. Huang took Chang'an and, after initially living at Tian's mansion and then moving into the palace, declared himself the emperor of a new state of Qi.

During Emperor Xizong's first flight from Chang'an

Emperor Xizong's train first fled to Fengxiang Circuit (鳳翔, headquartered in modern Baoji, Shaanxi), where the former chancellor Zheng Tian was military governor. After authorizing Zheng to oversee the resistance operation against Huang Chao, Emperor Xizong further fled to Shannan West, and then, at Chen Jingxuan's invitation, to Xichuan. (It was on this flight from Chang'an that Tian Lingzi would offend Emperor Xizong's brother Li Jie the Prince of Shou — the future Emperor Zhaozong, as during the flight, there was a time when Li Jie, then 13, became exhausted as the imperial train was going through rugged terrain on foot. He requested that Tian give him a horse, and Tian responded, "We are in high mountains. Where can we find horses?" Tian then hit the prince with a whip and ordered him to continue, causing Li Jie to bear a deep grudge against him.)

Once the imperial train arrived at Xichuan's capital Chengdu, however, Tian quickly alienated the Xichuan troops by giving great rewards to the imperial guard soldiers that followed Emperor Xizong to Chengdu, while not sharing those rewards with Xichuan troops. After the officer Guo Qi (郭琪) complained, Tian tried to poison Guo to death, but failed. Guo responded by starting a mutiny, but his mutiny was quickly defeated. When the advisory official Meng Zhaotu (孟昭圖) submitted a petition that urged Emperor Xizong to not just consult with Tian and Chen on the affairs of state but to listen to advice from the chancellors, Tian suppressed Meng's petition, exiled Meng, and had Meng killed in exile, to stifle criticism. Subsequently, when the lead chancellor Wang Duo was put in charge of the overall operations against Huang but was initially unsuccessful until Wang adopted the suggestion by the eunuch monitor Yang Fuguang to enlist the aid of the Shatuo chieftain Li Keyong, Tian used this as excuse, in spring 883, after the imperial forces defeated Huang and caused Huang to abandon Chang'an, to remove Wang as the commander of the operations against Huang. Further, he persuaded the chancellors and the regional governors to submit petitions to Emperor Xizong praising Tian himself of his contributions, and therefore Emperor Xizong made Tian the commander of all imperial guards. Later in the year, after Yang Fuguang died, Tian used the opportunity to remove Yang Fuguang's cousin Yang Fugong from his post as director of palace communications. Meanwhile, Zheng Tian, who by this point was at Chengdu and serving as chancellor, was not willing to simply agree with Tian's and Chen's requests, and Tian reacted by encouraging Li Changyan (a subordinate of Zheng's who had expelled Zheng from Fengxiang in 881) to threaten not to allow Zheng through Fengxiang when Emperor Xizong would be returning to Chang'an. Zheng was forced to resign and retire to Peng Prefecture (彭州, in modern Chengdu).

Meanwhile, Tian and Chen had also alienated Yang Shili by promising to make another general, Gao Renhou, the military governor of Dongchuan. Tian tried to preempt any actions Yang might take by summoning Yang to Chengdu in spring 884. Yang reacted by openly declaring a campaign against Tian and Chen. Gao subsequently waged a campaign against Yang, putting Dongchuan's capital Zi Prefecture (梓州) under siege. Yang's subordinate Zheng Junxiong (鄭君雄) then killed Yang and surrendered.

By this point, one of the former subordinates of Yang Fuguang's, Lu Yanhong, had seized Shannan West Circuit. Tian enticed Lu's subordinates Wang Jian, Han Jian, Zhang Zao (張造), Jin Hui (晉暉), and Li Shitai (李師泰) to abandon Lu and flee to him. Tian then adopted the five of them as sons, and put them directly under his command without incorporating them into the imperial guard command structure. He then attacked Lu, and Lu abandoned Shannan West and fled. Subsequently, in spring 885, with Tian escorting him, Emperor Xizong finally returned to Chang'an, yet Tian continued to be in control of the governance.

During and after Emperor Xizong's second flight from Chang'an

Once the imperial train returned to Chang'an, however, the imperial government was caught in a major financial crunch — as, in the aftermaths of Huang Chao's rebellion, the circuits became far more independent from the imperial government than ever, and were not submitting their tax revenues to the imperial government, which was only receiving such remittance from Chang'an and the surrounding regions. As Tian Lingzi greatly expanded the Shence Armies during the time Emperor Xizong was in Xichuan, the imperial government was unable to pay for all of the soldiers' and officials' salaries. Tian tried to remedy the situation by ordering the control of the salt pools in Hezhong Circuit (河中, headquartered in modern Yuncheng, Shanxi) be returned to the imperial government so that the revenues could be restored. The military governor of Hezhong, Wang Chongrong, did not want to give up the salt pools, and submitted repeated petitions opposing the order. The situation was further exacerbated when Tian sent his adoptive son Tian Kuangyou (田匡祐) to Hezhong as an emissary, as, while Wang initially received Tian Kuangyou with respect, Tian Kuangyou's arrogance offended the Hezhong soldiers. Wang thereafter publicly denounced Tian Kuangyou and Tian Lingzi, and it was only at the intercession of the Hezhong eunuch monitor that Wang allowed Tian Kuangyou to leave Hezhong. When Tian Kuangyou returned to Chang'an, he urged Tian Lingzi to take action against Wang. In summer 885, Tian had Emperor Xizong issue an edict transferring Wang to Taining Circuit (泰寧, headquartered in modern Jining, Shandong), Taining's military governor Qi Kerang to Yiwu Circuit (義武, headquartered in modern Baoding, Hebei), and Yiwu's military governor Wang Chucun to Hezhong. Wang Chongrong, incensed, refused to report to Taining and aligned himself with Li Keyong, who had then become the military governor of Hedong Circuit (河東, headquartered in modern Taiyuan, Shanxi). He also submitted a petition denouncing Tian Lingzi for 10 crimes. (Wang Chucun also tried to intercede on Wang Chongrong's behalf, but Tian did not relent.) Tian, in turn, aligned himself with Li Changyan's brother Li Changfu (who had succeeded Li Changyan as the military governor of Fengxiang after Li Changyan's death in 884) and Zhu Mei the military governor of Jingnan Circuit (靜難, headquartered in modern Xianyang, Shaanxi).

The Shence Army soldiers rendezvoused with the Jingnan and Fengxiang soldiers, and they attacked Hezhong. Wang Chongrong and Li Keyong then joined forces and engaged the Shence/Jingnan/Fengxiang armies at Shayuan (沙苑, in modern Weinan, Shaanxi) in winter 885. The Hezhong/Hedong forces prevailed, and after the defeat, Zhu and Li Changfu fled back to their own circuits. Li Keyong headed toward Chang'an. Tian escorted Emperor Xizong and fled to Fengxiang. Tian then, against Emperor Xizong's wishes, forced Emperor Xizong to further flee to Shannan West's capital Xingyuan (興元). It was said that, by this point, the people of the realm were thoroughly disgusted with Tian, and Zhu and Li Changfu, ashamed of aligning with him, also turned against him, and sent soldiers to chase after Emperor Xizong. They were not, however, and the imperial guards subsequently took control of Xingyuan, forcing Zhu's ally Shi Junshe (石君涉) to flee. Meanwhile, Zhu captured Emperor Xizong's distant relative Li Yun the Prince of Xiang and had Li Yun declared emperor at Chang'an. Facing universal condemnation, Tian recommended Yang Fugong to succeed him and commissioned himself as the eunuch monitor of the Xichuan army, and subsequently left for Xichuan.

By 887, Zhu had been killed by his own subordinate Wang Xingyu, and Wang Chongrong killed Li Yun. Emperor Xizong was thus able to return to Chang'an. He issued an edict stripping Tian of all of his titles and exiling Tian to Duan Prefecture (端州, in modern Zhaoqing, Guangdong). However, as Tian was then under Chen Jingxuan's protection, the exile order was never carried out.

Meanwhile, Tian's former subordinate and adoptive son Wang Jian had taken his soldiers and made them into a band of roving raiders, loosely aligned with Gu Yanlang the military governor of Dongchuan. Chen feared that Wang and Gu would join their forces and attack Xichuan. Tian suggested that he try to summon Wang to join the Xichuan army, and Chen agreed. Tian did so in winter 887, but subsequently, as Wang was marching toward Xichuan in response to Tian's summons, Chen's subordinate Li Ai (李乂) persuaded him that Wang would be dangerous to have in his realm. Chen thereafter tried to stop Wang from further advancing. Wang, in anger, defeated soldiers that Chen sent to try to stop him, and marched all the way to Chengdu. When Tian went onto the city walls to try to resolve the situation, Wang bowed to him but stated that since the situation left him with nowhere to go, he would be truly a rebel fro this point on. Wang put Chengdu under siege, but was unable to immediately capture it. Emperor Xizong sent emissaries to try to mediate the situation, but neither Chen nor Wang accepted the mediation.

During Emperor Zhaozong's reign

Emperor Xizong died in spring 888, and Li Jie, with Yang Fugong's support, became emperor (as Emperor Zhaozong). Meanwhile, Wang Jian submitted a petition to the new emperor condemning Chen Jingxuan and offering to serve as an assistant to any general that the imperial government might commission to replace Chen. Gu Yanlang also submitted a petition requesting that Chen be transferred. Emperor Zhaozong, who still bore a grudge against Tian, decided to accept Wang and Gu's proposal. He commissioned the chancellor Wei Zhaodu as the military governor of Xichuan to replace Chen and summoned Chen back to Chang'an to serve as a general of the imperial guards. When Chen refused, he declared Chen a renegade and ordered Wei, Wang, and Gu to attack.

The imperial campaign against Chen, however, stalled, despite the joint forces' putting Chengdu under siege. By 891 Emperor Zhaozong's officials had become convinced that it would not succeed. Emperor Zhaozong therefore issued an edict restoring Chen's titles and ordering Gu and Wang (whom Emperor Zhaozong had given the title of military governor of a newly carved out Yongping Circuit (永平, headquartered in modern Chengdu at nearby Qiong Prefecture (邛州)) to return to their own posts. Wang, believing that success was imminent, instead intimidated Wei into surrendering his army to Wang and returning to Chang'an. Wang took control of the army and continued the intense attacks on Chengdu, while sending parts of the army to capture the other cities of Xichuan. Wang also cut off supplies that Yang Sheng was sending from Peng Prefecture (彭州, in modern Chengdu) to Chengdu.

In fall 888, desperate, Tian conversed

with Wang from the top of the city walls. Wang promised that he would continue to treat Tian as a father if Chen surrendered. That night, Tian went to Wang's camp and formally surrendered Chen's seals. Wang accepted, and apologized to Tian, asking that the father-son relationship be restored. Wang took control of Xichuan. He commissioned Chen's son Chen Tao (陳陶) as the prefect of Ya Prefecture (雅州, in modern Ya'an, Sichuan) and had Chen Jingxuan accompany his son to Ya Prefecture. Meanwhile, he kept Tian under house arrest in Chengdu.

Despite Wang's declaration that he would honor Tian again as father, he was repeatedly submitting petitions to the imperial government to order the executions of Chen Jingxuan and Tian. The imperial government never did so, however, and in summer 893 Wang decided to take things into his own hands. Accusing Chen of plotting a rebellion, he put Chen to death. He also accused Tian of communicating with Fengxiang's then-military governor Li Maozhen (whom Tian had treated well before while Li Maozhen served at the Shence Armies and who had tried to intercede on Tian's behalf) and put Tian to death. As he was facing death, Tian tore apart linen strips and stated to the executioner, "I had previously overseen the 10 armies [(i.e., the imperial guards)]. You need to kill me properly." He then showed the executioner how he could be strangled with the linen, and the executioner did so. Later, during the middle of Emperor Zhaozong's Qianning era (894-898), for reasons unclear, Tian's titles were posthumously restored.

Source (edited): "http://en.wikipedia.org/wiki/Tian_Lingzi"

Tutu Chengcui

Tutu Chengcui (吐突承璀) (died 820), courtesy name **Renzhen** (仁貞), was a powerful eunuch of the Chinese dynasty Tang Dynasty, during the reign of Emperor Xianzong.

Background

It is not known when Tutu Chengcui was born — or whether he was originally surnamed Tutu, although, as it is known that he was from the Min region (閩, roughly modern Fujian), it would appear doubtful, as Tutu was largely a Xianbei surname. Early in his career as an eunuch, he served at the eastern palace (i.e., the Crown Prince's palace) and later served as a supervising eunuch at the textile agency (掖庭局, Yiting Ju) within the eunuch bureau (內侍省, Neishi Sheng). It was said that he was dextrous, intelligent, and capable. While he was serving at the Crown Prince's palace, he served under Li Chun the Prince of Guangling, a son of then-crown prince Li Song (who was a son of then-reigning Emperor Dezong).

During Emperor Xianzong's reign

In 805, Emperor Dezong died, and Li Song became emperor (as Emperor Shunzong), but as Emperor Shunzong was himself severely ill at that point, he yielded the throne to Li Chun later in the year (as Emperor Xianzong). Emperor Xianzong made Tutu Chengcui Neichangshi (內常侍) — the secretary general of the eunuch bureau, serving as the acting head of the eunuch bureau. In 806, Tutu was also made the commander (中尉, Zhongwei) of the Left Shence Army (左神策軍), as well as the director of religious affairs (功德使, Gongdeshi).

In 809, one of the key military governors (Jiedushi) who had been ruling their circuits in a de facto independent manner — Wang Shizhen the military governor of Chengde Circuit (成德, headquartered in modern Shijiazhuang, Hebei) — died. Wang Shizhen's son Wang Chengzong declared himself acting military governor. In the past, these successions were routinely approved by the imperial government, but Emperor Xianzong, wanting to reassert imperial authority, hesitated in doing so and considered taking the control of Chengde back by force. The chancellor Pei Ji opposed military action, but Tutu volunteered to command an army against Wang Chengzong. Meanwhile, Lu Congshi (盧從史) the military governor of Zhaoyi Circuit (昭義, headquartered in modern Changzhi, Shanxi) wanted imperial favor, and offered, through Tutu, to attack Wang as well, causing Emperor Xianzong to consider military action further.

Meanwhile, around the same time, there was an incident where Tutu, in his role as director of religious affairs, remodeled Anguo Temple (安國寺) and, in the process, built a magnificent stele and asked for Emperor Xianzong to designate an official to author the text of the stele, to praise Emperor Xianzong. Emperor Xianzong asked the imperial scholar Li Jiang to do so, but Li Jiang pointed out that of the great rulers of antiquity, none erected monuments to praise himself, and the poorly-regarded Qin Shi Huang did. Emperor Xianzong thus ordered Tutu to destroy the stele.

To resolve the standoff, Wang Chengzong offered to surrender two of Chengde's six prefectures — De (德州, in modern Dezhou, Shandong) and Di (棣州, in modern Binzhou, Shandong) — to imperial control as a new Baoxin Circuit. Emperor Xianzong was set to accept the offer and make Wang military governor, but Wang soon retracted the offer and arrested Xue Changchao (薛昌朝), whom Emperor Xianzong was set to commission as the military governor of Baoxin. In winter 809, Emperor Xianzong stripped Wang of his titles and commissioned Tutu as the commander of the forces against Chengde. Many officials, including Bai Juyi, Li Yuansu (李元素), Li Yong, Xu Mengrong (許孟容), Li Yijian, Meng Jian (孟簡), Lü Yuanying (呂元膺), Mu Zhi (穆質), and Dugu Yu (獨孤郁), opposed the commission, arguing that generals would feel ashamed serving under a eunuch. Emperor Xianzong reduced Tutu's title slightly but kept him in command.

In spring 810, Tutu arrived at the northern front against Chengde, but it was said that he lacked the respect of the generals, and the military actions were therefore less than successful. In particular, after one key imperial general, Li Dingjin (酈定進) was killed in battle, the morale took a major blow. Meanwhile, Tutu and Emperor Xianzong became aware that while Lu Congshi had initially encouraged military action against Chengde, he was actually secretly in communications with Chengde and interfering with the military action. Tutu thus befriended Lu by giving Lu various treasures as gifts. Once Lu's guard was down, on one occasion when Lu was at Tutu's headquarters, Tutu had him arrested and had Lu's subordinate Wu Chongyin take control of the Zhaoyi army. Tutu subsequently recommended Wu to succeed Lu, but at the suggestion of Li Jiang, Emperor Xianzong made Wu the military governor of Heyang Circuit (河陽, headquartered in modern Luoyang, Henan) and made Meng Yuanyang (孟元陽) the military governor of Heyang Circuit the new military governor of Zhaoyi. After Lu's arrest, Wang submitted a petition offering to submit and accusing Lu of having alienated him from the imperial government. As imperial forces were having no success against Wang by that point, Emperor Xianzong recalled Tutu's army and exonerated Wang and his soldiers, making Wang the military governor of Chengde.

After Tutu returned to the capital Chang'an, Emperor Xianzong initially had him resume the command of the Left Shence Army. However, Pei, Duan Pingzhong (段平仲), Lü, and Li Jiang all advocated that, because Tutu was unable to defeat Wang as he promised, he should be punished. Emperor Xianzong, in response, demoted Tutu to be the director of armory supplies (軍器使, *Junqishi*). It was said that people celebrated Tutu's demotion.

In 811, Tutu's subordinate Liu Xiguang (劉希光) was found to have received bribes from the general Sun Rui (孫璹) to help make Sun a military governor. Liu was forced to commit suicide, and during the investigation, Tutu was implicated. Emperor Xianzong thus demoted Tutu out of the capital to serve as the monitoring eunuch at Huainan Circuit (淮南, headquartered in modern Yangzhou, Jiangsu).

While Tutu was at Huainan, Li Yong served as military governor. It was said that while Li Yong was strict and stern, he and Tutu respected each other and did not interfere with each other. Meanwhile, in 814, with Li Jiang, who was then chancellor, repeatedly offering to resign due to a foot illness, Emperor Xianzong removed Li Jiang from his chancellor position and made him the minister of rites, with an eye toward recalling Tutu after that. He soon did so, and Tutu was again made the director of armory supplies as well as the commander of the Left Shence Army. Appreciative of the mutual respect that he had with Li Yong, in 817, he recommended Li Yong to be chancellor, and Emperor Xianzong thus recalled Li Yong to be chancellor. However, Li Yong found it shameful to be recommended by a eunuch, and upon arrival in Chang'an, he offered to resign and refused to meet his subordinates as chancellor or to carry out the duties of chancellor. Emperor Xianzong made Li Yijian chancellor instead. Meanwhile, in 818, also at Tutu's recommendation, Emperor Xianzong made Huangfu Bo a chancellor as well.

Death

Meanwhile, Tutu Chengcui also injected himself into Emperor Xianzong's succession plans. Emperor Xianzong had initially, in 809, created his oldest son Li Ning, who was not born of his wife Consort Guo, crown prince, but Li Ning died in 811. After Li Ning's death, Tutu suggested that Emperor Xianzong's next oldest son, Li Kuan (李寬) the Prince of Li (whose name was later changed to Li Yun (李惲)), be created crown prince. Emperor Xianzong disagreed and created Consort Guo's son Li You the Prince of Sui (whose name was soon changed to Li Heng) crown prince instead. Despite this, Tutu continued to advocate for Li Yun's ascension, particularly after his recall. In 820, when Emperor Xianzong grew ill, it was said that Tutu was plotting to have Li Yun become emperor, such that Li Heng feared for his own safety.

In spring 820, Emperor Xianzong died suddenly — and historians generally believed that it was the eunuch Chen Hongzhi (陳弘志) who murdered him. The eunuchs Liang Shouqian (梁守謙), Ma Jintan (馬進潭), Liu Chengjie (劉承偕), Wei Yuansu (韋元素), and Wang Shoucheng, had Tutu and Li Yun killed, and they supported Li Heng to succeed to the throne (as Emperor Muzong). During the reign of Emperor Muzong's son Emperor Jingzong, the eunuch Ma Cunliang (馬存亮) submitted a petition listing the accomplishments of Tutu, and Emperor Jingzong allowed Tutu's adopted son Tutu Shiye (吐突士曄) to have Tutu Chengcui reburied properly. During the subsequent reign of another of son of Emperor Xianzong's, Emperor Xuānzong, Tutu Shiye was further promoted to be commander of the Right Shence Army (右神策軍).

Source (edited): "http://en.wikipedia.org/wiki/Tutu_Chengcui"

Wang Shoucheng

Wang Shoucheng (王守澄) (died November 3, 835) was a powerful eunuch of the Chinese dynasty Tang Dynasty, wielding substantial powers during the reigns of Emperor Xianzong, Emperor Muzong, Emperor Jingzong, and Emperor Wenzong. By 835, however, two non-eunuchs that he had recommended to Emperor Wenzong — Li Xun and Zheng Zhu — were plotting with Emperor Wenzong to exterminate the eunuchs, and as part of the plan, Emperor Wenzong sent poison to Wang and ordered him to commit suicide.

During Emperor Xianzong's reign

Both Wang Shoucheng's birthdate and geographic origins have been lost to history. The earliest historical records of his activities indicated that during the reign of Emperor Xianzong, when the general Li Su served as the military governor (*Jiedushi*) of Wuning Circuit (武寧, headquartered in modern Xuzhou, Jiangsu), Wang served as the eunuch monitor of the Wuning army. While both Wang and Li were at Wuning, one of Li's subordinates introduced Li to the physician Zheng Zhu, as Li was frequently ill. Li was helped by Zheng's medicines, and subsequently, Zheng took substantial power at the Wuning headquarters. At the other officers' requests, Wang requested that Li remove Zheng. Li admitted that Zheng was frivolous, but indicated that Zheng was witty and engaging in talk. At Li's insistence, Wang met Zheng, and soon was also impressed by Zheng's wit; he was also helped by Zheng's medicines as well. Zheng thereafter became a close associate of Wang's.

By 820, Wang was back in the capital Chang'an and serving in the palace. That spring, Emperor Xianzong died suddenly — traditionally believed to be in an assassination by the eunuch Chen Hongzhi (陳弘志), although Wang's biography in the *New Book of Tang* indicated that Wang was also involved in the assassination. In the aftermaths of Emperor Xianzong's death, the powerful eunuch Tutu Chengcui tried to support Emperor Xianzong's oldest surviving son Li Yun (李惲) the Prince of Li as emperor, but other eunuchs, including Wang, Liang Shouqian (梁守謙), Ma Jintan (馬進潭), Liu Chengjie (劉承偕), and Wei Yuansu (韋元素) supported another son of Emperor Xianzong's, the Crown Prince Li Heng, and they killed Tutu and Li Yun. Li Heng subsequently took the throne (as Emperor Muzong).

During Emperor Muzong's reign

During Emperor Muzong's reign, Wang Shoucheng became one of the two palace secretaries general (樞密使, *Shumishi*). He was said to be very powerful and involved in affairs of state, such that in 823, the official Zheng Quan (鄭權) was able to beg Wang through Zheng Zhu and be made the military governor of Lingnan Circuit (嶺南, headquartered in modern Guangzhou, Guangdong). Wang was also in an alliance with the chancellor Li Fengji.

During Emperor Jingzong's reign

In 824, Emperor Muzong died and was succeeded by his son Emperor Jingzong. Li Fengji subsequently had Wang Shoucheng report to Emperor Jingzong that their political enemy, the imperial scholar Li Shen (李紳), had wanted to support Emperor Muzong's younger brother Li Cong (李悰) the Prince of Shen instead of Emperor Jingzong. As a result, Li Shen was exiled.

During Emperor Jingzong's reign, Wang remained highly influential in policy decisions. For example, in 825, it was said that it was at the decision of Li Fengji and Wang that, after the death of Liu Wu the military governor of Zhaoyi Circuit (昭義, headquartered in modern Changzhi, Shanxi) that Liu Wu's son Liu Congjian was allowed to inherit Zhaoyi Circuit.

In 826, Emperor Jingzong was assassinated by his polo player Su Zuoming (蘇佐明). The eunuch Liu Keming (劉克明) supported Emperor Muzong's younger brother Li Wu the Prince of Jiàng, and at one point, Li Wu was meeting with the officials and acting as if he would be the next emperor. However, Wang and other powerful eunuchs, including Yang Chenghe (楊承和), Wei Congjian (魏從簡), and Liang Shouqian, soon mobilized their troops and attacked Liu's party. Liu committed suicide, while Li Wu was killed. They supported Emperor Jingzong's younger brother Li Han the Prince of Jiāng (note different tone), who changed his name to Li Ang, as emperor (as Emperor Wenzong). It was Wang who consulted with the imperial scholar Wei Chuhou to deal with the ceremony of Emperor Wenzong's enthronement after the coup.

During Emperor Wenzong's reign

After Emperor Wenzong's enthronement, Wang Shoucheng was given the honorific title of *Piaoqi Dajiangjun* (驃騎大將軍) and made the commander of the Right Shence Army (右神策軍). As time went by, Emperor Wenzong came to be apprehensive that those he believed to be involved in Emperors Xianzong's and Jingzong's death were still in the palace, and, in particular, he became displeased at Wang's hold on politics and open receptions of bribery. He began to discuss a way to counteract Wang with the imperial scholar Song Shenxi, and in 830 made Song chancellor. After Song involved Wang Fan (王璠) the mayor of Jingzhao Municipality (京兆, i.e., the Chang'an region) in 831, however, Wang Fan leaked the plan, and Wang Shoucheng and Zheng Zhu came to know about the plan. Zheng reacted by ordering the Shence Army officer Doulu Zhu (豆盧著) to falsely accuse Song of plotting treason to put Emperor Wenzong's younger brother Li Cou the Prince of Zhang on the throne. When Wang Shoucheng relayed the accusation to Emperor Wenzong, Emperor Wenzong believed it and was angry. Wang Shoucheng initially wanted to take this opportunity to massacre Song's household, but was stopped by another powerful eunuch, Ma Cunliang (馬存亮). However, during the subsequent investigations by Shence Army officers, after an attendant official to the imperial princes, Yan Jingze (晏敬則), and Song's associate Wang Shiwen (王師文) were tortured and confessed to serving as conduits for messages between Song and Li Cou, Song was found to be guilty and was set to be executed. The advisorial officials Cui Xuanliang (崔玄亮), Li Guyan, Wang Zhi (王質), Lu Jun (盧均), Shu Yuanbao (舒元褒), Jiang Xi (蔣係), Pei Xiu (裴休), and Wei Wen (韋溫) urged caution, however, believed there were substantial questions in the matter and urged a reinvestigation by imperial government officials. The chancellor Niu Sengru also took the same view. Zheng, fearing that a reinvestigation would lead to discovery of the truth, suggested to Wang Shoucheng that he recommend to Emperor Wenzong that neither Song nor Li Cou be executed. Li Cou was thus demoted to the title of Duke of Chao County (巢縣, in modern Chaohu, Anhui) while Song was demoted to be the military advisor to the prefect of Kai Prefecture (開州, in modern Chongqing).

Emperor Wenzong was, by this point, finding Wang Shoucheng's and Zheng's relationship to be distasteful, but after Emperor Wenzong suffered a stroke in 833, Wang recommended Zheng for his medical abilities, and after Emperor Wenzong was helped by Zheng's medicines, he began to favor Zheng as well. Around the same time, Zheng also introduced Li Zhongyan to Wang and Emperor Wenzong. Both became close associates of Emperor Wenzong's, and Li Zhongyan was made an imperial scholar over the objection of the chancellor Li Deyu, who was subsequently demoted out of the capital.

In 835, Emperor Wenzong was again discussing the matter of killing powerful eunuchs, this time with Zheng and Li Zhongyan — as he believed that, since Zheng and Li Zhongyan were recommended by Wang, they would not draw the suspicions from the eunuchs. At their suggestion, Emperor Wenzong first diverted some of Wang's authority by giving the command of the Left Shence Army (左神策軍) to Wang's rival among the eunuchs, Qiu Shiliang, displacing Wang's ally Wei Yuansu, in 835. Subsequently, Zheng and Li Zhongyan (whose name had been changed to Li Xun by this point) had Wei, Yang Chenghe, and another eunuch, Wang Jianyan (王踐言), sent out of Chang'an to serve as army monitors, and also had two other chancellors, Lu Sui and Li Zongmin, demoted. Later that year, Wang Shoucheng was given the high title of the supreme monitor of the Left and Right Shence Armies and supreme commander of the 12 imperial guard corps — in order for Emperor Wenzong to strip him of the command of the Right Shence Army. Soon thereafter, at Zheng's and Li Xun's suggestion, Emperor Wenzong sent the eunuch Li Haogu (李好古) to Wang's mansion with poison, ordering Wang to commit suicide. However, publicly, Emperor Wenzong did not allow the details be known, and posthumously honored Wang. Zheng and Li Xun thereafter planned to use Wang's funeral as the occasion to trap the eunuchs and massacre them, but Li Xun, wanting all the credit by himself, preempted the plan, but failed, in what later became known as the Ganlu Incident, leading to the eunuchs' massacre of four chancellors (in addition to Li Xun, who was chancellor by this point, Wang Ya, Jia Su, and Shu Yuanyu) and governmental officials.
Source (edited): "http://en.wikipedia.org/wiki/Wang_Shoucheng"

Yang Fugong

This is a Chinese name; the family name is Yang.

Yang Fugong (楊復恭) (died 894), courtesy name **Zike** (子恪), formally the **Duke of Wei** (魏公), was an eunuch official of the Chinese dynasty Tang Dynasty, playing key roles in the imperial administrations of Emperor Xizong and Emperor Xizong's brother Emperor Zhaozong. He was later suspected by Emperor Zhaozong of power-grabbing and removed, and afterwards encouraged his adoptive sons/nephews Yang Shouliang, Yang Shouxin (楊守信), Yang Shouzhen (楊守貞), and Yang Shouzhong (楊守忠) into resisting the imperial government together. They were, however, defeated by the general Li Maozhen and captured while in flight; they were then delivered to the capital Chang'an and executed.

Background

It is not known when Yang Fugong was born. He was originally surnamed Lin (林) until he, who apparently became an eunuch in his youth, became an adoptive son of the eunuch Yang Xuanyi (楊玄翼), who was a director of the palace communications (樞密使, *Shumishi*) during the middle of Emperor Yizong's *Xiantong* era (860-874). (He was thus adoptive cousin of another later-prominent eunuch, Yang Fuguang, who was the adoptive son of Yang Xuanyi's adoptive brother Yang Xuanjie (楊玄价).) Yang Fugong was literate and well-learned, and subsequently successively served as a eunuch monitor for several imperial armies. During the Pang Xun rebellion of 868-869, Yang Fugong served as the eunuch monitor of the Heyang Circuit (河陽, headquartered in modern Luoyang, Henan), and after Pang's rebellion was suppressed, Yang was credited and recalled to the capital Chang'an to serve as the palace-government liaison (宣徽使, *Xuanhuishi*). After Yang Xuanyi died in 870, Yang Fugong left governmental service for some time to observe a mourning period for him, but soon was recalled to serve as a director of palace communications.

During Emperor Xizong's reign

As of 880, when Emperor Yizong's son Emperor Xizong was emperor, Yang Fugong's colleague Tian Lingzi was extremely powerful due to his personal relationship with Emperor Xizong. When the agrarian rebel Huang Chao was approaching Chang'an, Yang Fugong served as Tian's deputy when Tian was commanding the imperial Shence Armies (神策軍), traditionally commanded by eunuchs. Subsequently, under Tian's advice, Emperor Xizong abandoned Chang'an and fled to Chengdu, where Tian's brother Chen Jingxuan served as the military governor (*Jiedushi*) of Xichuan Circuit (西川). It was said that due to Tian's control of the government, few dared to argue with him on policies, but Yang Fugong dared to, apparently partly because Yang Fugong's cousin Yang Fuguang then was in charge of one of the major Tang armies fighting against Huang (who had declared himself the emperor of a new state of Qi). After Yang Fuguang died in 883, however, Tian immediately had Yang Fugong demoted to be the director of the imperial stable (飛龍使, *Feilongshi*). Yang Fugong thus claimed to be ill and retired to his own mansion in Lantian (藍田, in modern Xi'an, Shaanxi).

In 885, by which time Huang's rebellion had been suppressed and Emperor Xizong had returned to Chang'an, Tian provoked the warlord Wang Chongrong (the military governor of Hezhong Circuit (河中, headquartered in modern Yuncheng, Shanxi)) by ordering Wang's transfer. Wang reacted by aligning himself with Li Keyong the military governor of Hedong Circuit (河東, headquartered in modern Taiyuan, Shanxi), and Wang and Li Keyong's troops defeated those of Tian and Tian's allies Li Changfu the military governor of Fengxiang Circuit (鳳翔, headquartered in modern Baoji, Shaanxi) and Zhu Mei the military governor of Jingnan Circuit (靜難, headquartered in modern Xianyang, Shaanxi). Tian again took Emperor Xizong and fled Chang'an, to Xingyuan (興元, in modern Hanzhong, Shaanxi). It was during this flight that Emperor Xizong made Yang Fugong the director of palace communications again, and soon thereafter, when Tian realized that he was open to condemnation from all sides (with his allies Li Changfu and Zhu having abandoned him, and Zhu going as far as supporting Emperor Xizong's distant relative Li Yun the Prince of Xiang as an alternative claimant to the imperial throne), Tian recommended Yang Fugong to succeed him, while making himself the eunuch monitor of Xichuan so that he could join his brother Chen. Subsequently, because of the friendship that Wang had with Yang Fuguang when both were fighting Huang, Yang Fugong was able to persuade Wang and Li Keyong to resubmit to Emperor Xizong.

Meanwhile, with Zhu's campaign against Emperor Xizong stalled, Yang issued a declaration to the Guanzhong region (i.e., the greater Chang'an region) that anyone who killed Zhu would be made the military governor of Jingnan. After hearing the declaration, Zhu's officer Wang Xingyu turned against him, launched a surprise attack on Chang'an (where Zhu and Li Yun were), and killed Zhu. Li Yun fled to Hezhong and was killed by Wang Chongrong, and his competing claim was extinguished. Subsequently, on the imperial train's return to Chang'an, Emperor Xizong stopped at Fengxiang, when a ceremonial dispute erupted between Li Changfu and Yang's adoptive son Yang Shouli (楊守立). This erupted into open battle between the Fengxiang army and imperial guards. The imperial guard general Li Maozhen was able to defeat Li Changfu and force him to flee; Li Changfu was subsequently killed by his own subordinate Xue Zhichou (薛知籌), and Li Maozhen took Fengxiang. Upon Emperor Xizong's return to Chang'an, for Yang Fugong's contributions, he was created the Duke of Wei.

In spring 888, Emperor Xizong grew seriously ill. It was said that most imperial officials hoped that his brother Li Bao (李保) the Prince of Ji, who was considered capable, would succeed him, but that under Yang Fugong's support, another brother of Emperor Xizong's, Li Jie the Prince of Shou, was created the Crown Prince. When Emperor Xizong died soon thereafter, Li Jie (whose name was then changed to Li Min) took the throne (as Emperor Zhaozong).

During Emperor Zhaozong's reign

Because of Yang Fugong's contributions to Emperor Zhaozong's taking the throne, he tried to exert his influence in policy decisions, gradually drawing Emperor Zhaozong's displeasure. He further offended the emperor by being arrogant, including riding a litter all the way into the palace, and adopting many strong military officers to be his sons. This caused both the chancellor Kong Wei and Emperor Zhaozong to openly accuse him of impropriety, and Yang, while initially responding that he adopted many officers in order to help defend the emperor, was unable to respond when Emperor Zhaozong pointed out that those officers, then, should be adopted into the imperial clan of Li rather than Yang's own clan. (Indeed, Emperor Zhaozong subsequently demanded to have Yang Shouli attend to him, and Yang Fugong had to accede to the emperor's wishes; Emperor Zhaozong then bestowed a new name, Li Shunjie (李順節), on Yang Shouli, and made him a commander of his personal guards.)

Meanwhile, Yang Fugong had a deep enmity with the chancellor Zhang Jun — because he had initially recommended Zhang for imperial service, but Zhang, after Yang Fugong's initial retirement, immediately became a follower of Yang's rival Tian Lingzi. Emperor Zhaozong, because of this enmity between Zhang and Yang Fugong, further trusted Zhang in order to counteract Yang. As of 890, Zhang, who had also been displeased with Li Keyong because Li Keyong had criticized him, persuaded Emperor Zhaozong to declare a general campaign against Li Keyong, supported by Li Keyong's rival warlords Zhu Quanzhong the military governor of Xuanwu Circuit (宣武, headquartered in modern Kaifeng, Henan) and Li Kuangwei the military governor of Lulong Circuit (盧龍, headquartered in modern Beijing) but opposed by Yang. Zhang's campaign, however, was unsuccessful, purportedly partly due to Yang's sabotage. After Li Keyong defeated the imperial forces, he demanded that Zhang and Kong (who agreed with Zhang's proposal) be demoted. The two were exiled.

Yang continued to exert influence over the imperial governance, and many of his adoptive sons and nephews became powerful generals, including his adoptive sons Yang Shouzhen the military governor of Longjian Circuit (龍劍, headquartered in Mianyang, Sichuan) and Yang Shouzhong the military governor of Wuding Circuit (武定,

headquartered in modern Hanzhong), as well as Yang Fuguang's adoptive son Yang Shouliang the military governor of Shannan West Circuit (山南西道, headquartered in modern Hanzhong as well (at Xingyuan)). Yang Fugong also developed another enmity, with Emperor Zhaozong's maternal uncle Wang Gui (王瓌). In fall 891, Yang thus recommended Wang to be the military governor of Qiannan Circuit (黔南). (Where Qiannan was is unclear; the modern historian Bo Yang believed that it was a fictional circuit that Yang created for the sole purpose of murdering Wang.) As Wang was heading to his post through Shannan West, Yang had Yang Shouliang send soldiers disguised as bandits to ambush Wang and kill his entire train. Emperor Zhaozong, believing Yang Fugong to be behind the killings, became hateful of Yang. Further, Li Shunjie, now with a direct relationship with the emperor, was informing the emperor of Yang's misdeeds. Emperor Zhaozong thus ordered Yang to be the eunuch monitor to Fengxiang, but Yang refused on account of illness. He thereafter ordered Yang's retirement, and Yang retired to his mansion at Lantian.

As Yang's mansion was close to the Yushan Camp (玉山營), Yang Fuguang's adoptive son Yang Shouxin, who commanded the Yushan Camp, visited him frequently, and thus rumors developed that Yang Fugong and Yang Shouxin were plotting treason. Emperor Zhaozong preemptively ordered Li Shunjie and another imperial guard officer, Li Shoujie (李守節), to attack Yang Fugong's mansion. Yang Fugong and Yang Shouxin took their families and fled to Xingyuan. There, he, Yang Shouliang, Yang Shouzhong, Yang Shouzhen, and another adoptive son, Yang Shouhou (楊守厚) the prefect of Mian Prefecture (綿州, in modern Mianyang), jointly announced a campaign, ostensibly against Li Shunjie.

The imperial government did not immediately engage the Yangs. However, in spring 892, five nearby military governors — Li Maozhen of Fengxiang, Wang Xingyu of Jingnan, Han Jian of Zhenguo Circuit (鎮國, headquartered in modern Weinan, Shaanxi), Wang Xingyue (王行約, Wang Xingyu's brother) of Kuangguo Circuit (匡國, headquartered in modern Weinan as well), and Li Maozhuang (李茂莊, Li Maozhen's brother) of Tianxiong (天雄, headquartered in modern Tianshui, Gansu) — apparently seeing this as an excellent opportunity to annex the Yangs' territory, submitted a joint petition requesting permission to attack the Yangs and requesting that Li Maozhen be put in command of the operations. Emperor Zhaozong, believing that if Li Maozhen took over the Yangs' territory, he would be even harder to control, ordered mediation, but no one accepted imperial mediation. Subsequently, Emperor Zhaozong felt compelled to agree with Li Maozhen's wishes, and so formally declared Li Maozhen the commander of the operations against the Yangs.

Li Maozhen quickly captured much of the Yangs' territory, and in fall 892, he captured Xingyuan, and put his adoptive son Li Jimi (李繼密) in acting command of Shannan West. Yang Fugong, along with Yang Shouliang, Yang Shouxin, Yang Shouzhen, Yang Shouzhong, and another follower, Man Cun (滿存), fled to Lang Prefecture (閬州, in modern Nanchong, Sichuan). In fall 894, Li Maozhen further attacked Lang Prefecture and captured it. Yang Fuguang, Yang Shouliang, and Yang Shouxin fought out of the encirclement and tried to flee toward Hedong. When they went through Zhenguo, however, Han's soldiers captured them. Han executed Yang Fugong and Yang Shouxin, and delivered their heads and Yang Shouliang to Chang'an, where Yang Shouliang was executed as well. Another adoptive son, Yang Yanbo (楊彥伯), did make it to Hedong. Apparently due to Yang Yanbo's request, Li Keyong submitted a petition in Yang Fugong's defense, and Yang Yanbo was permitted to bury Yang Fugong properly, and Yang Fugong's titles were subsequently restored posthumously.

Source (edited): "http://en.wikipedia.org/wiki/Yang_Fugong"

Yang Fuguang

This is a Chinese name; the family name is Yang.

Yang Fuguang (楊復光) (842-883), formally **Duke Zhongsu of Hongnong** (弘農忠肅公), was an eunuch general of the Chinese dynasty Tang Dynasty, who was considered a major contributor to the Tang cause in finally defeating Huang Chao's rebellion.

Background

Yang Fuguang was born in 842, during the reign of Emperor Wuzong. He was originally surnamed Qiao (喬) and was from the Min (閩) region — i.e., modern Fujian. At some point, he became an eunuch and an adoptive son of the powerful eunuch Yang Xuanjie (楊玄价), and therefore took the surname of Yang. It was said that Yang Fuguang was strong and self-motivated, impressing Yang Xuanjie. Because Yang Fuguang was considered to have military capabilities, he served several successive terms as eunuch monitor of armies. (Yang Fuguang was thus the adoptive cousin of another later-prominent eunuch, Yang Fugong, as Yang Fugong was the adoptive son of Yang Xuanjie's adoptive brother Yang Xuanyi (楊玄翼).)

During Emperor Xizong's reign

Before Huang Chao captured Chang'an

As of 876, Yang Fuguang was serving as the eunuch monitor of the army under the general Zeng Yuanyu (曾元裕), who was then serving as the deputy commander for Tang forces in the campaign against the agrarian rebel Wang Xianzhi. In 877, Yang sent messengers to Wang and persuaded him to surrender to Tang imperial forces. Wang agreed, and he sent his general Shang Junzhang (尚君長) to further discuss the matter with Yang. Zeng's superior Song Wei (宋威), however, ambushed and captured Shang on his way to Yang's camp. Song then submitted a report claiming that he had captured Shang in battle. Despite Yang's report that Shang was participating in Wang's negotiations to surrender, then-reigning Emperor Xizong believed Song's report and had Shang executed. In anger, Wang broke off negotiations and continued his rebellion. Subsequently, when the chancellor Wang Duo was put in overall command of the operations, Yang served as the eunuch monitor of his army.

By 880, when Wang Xianzhi had already been killed in battle but Huang Chao had in turn become the most powerful agrarian rebel figure, Yang Fuguang was serving as the eunuch monitor of Jingnan Circuit (荊南, headquartered in modern Jingzhou, Hubei), when, in the absence of a military governor (*Jiedushi*), he commissioned the officer Song Hao (宋浩) to oversee the circuit's affairs. Subsequently, though, when Song had a dispute with the officer Duan Yanmo over Song's punishment of some of Duan's soldiers, Duan killed Song. Yang subsequently submitted a report that indicated that Song's punishment was overly harsh, and Duan was not punished. (According to Yang's biography in the *New Book of Tang*, Yang encouraged Duan's actions because Song was disrespectful to Yang as well.) Subsequently, Yang was made the eunuch monitor at Zhongwu Circuit (忠武, headquartered in modern Xuchang, Henan).

After Huang Chao captured Chang'an

Late in 880, Huang Chao captured the imperial capital Chang'an, forcing Emperor Xizong to flee to Chengdu. A number of Tang generals submitted to Huang, who declared himself the emperor of a new state of Qi. Among those was the military governor of Zhongwu, Zhou Ji. One night, when Zhou invited Yang Fuguang to a feast, Yang's attendants, pointing out that Zhou had already submitted to Qi, Yang should fear whether Zhou would kill him. Yang pointed out that he needed to do what he could to persuade Zhou back to the Tang imperial cause and should do so despite dangers to himself, and so attended the feast. At the feast, Yang persuaded Zhou to rejoin the Tang cause, and he further sent his adoptive son Yang Shouliang to assassinate Huang's emissary to Zhongwu. Subsequently, Yang organized the Zhongwu troops into eight corps, commanded by eight officers, including Lu Yanhong, Jin Hui (晉暉), Wang Jian, Han Jian, Zhang Zao (張造), Li Shitai (李師泰), and Pang Cong (龐從). The Zhongwu forces were able to repel the Qi forces under Zhu Wen, preserving Zhongwu's ability to resist Qi. In winter 881, Yang further advanced his troops to Wugong (武功, in modern Xianyang, Shaanxi), close to Chang'an, preparing to participate in the operations to recapture Chang'an from Huang. Tang forces subsequently briefly recaptured Chang'an, but Huang subsequently defeated them and took Chang'an again. Yang subsequently joined forces with Wang Chongrong the military governor of Hezhong Circuit (河中, headquartered in modern Yuncheng, Shanxi), and they persuaded Zhu, who then was at Tong Prefecture (同州, in modern Weinan, Shaanxi), to join the Tang cause as well.

However, Huang's army remained powerful, and Wang was apprehensive to directly act against Huang. Yang suggested that they enlist the aid of the Shatuo chieftain Li Keyong — who had previously rebelled against Tang and been branded a renegade. Yang submitted the proposal to Wang Duo (who was then again overseeing the operations against Huang), and Wang issued an edict in Emperor Xizong's name summoning Li Keyong. Li Keyong agreed, and he joined forces with Yang and Wang Chongrong, preparing to again attack Chang'an. In summer 883, with Li Keyong leading the operation, the imperial forces defeated Huang's, forcing Huang to abandon Chang'an and flee east. Subsequently, it was Yang who submitted the public report to Emperor Xizong proclaiming the victory at Chang'an. For his contributions, he was given the honorific title of *Kaifu Yitong Sansi* (開府儀同三司) and created the Duke of Hongnong.

Yang died later in 883, at Hezhong. It was said that because he had led the troops well, the troops greatly mourned his death. Yang had a large number of adoptive sons (who were not eunuchs), and many of them would become key military officers.

Source (edited): "http://en.wikipedia.org/wiki/Yang_Fuguang"

Yu Chao'en

Yu Chao'en (魚朝恩) (722 – April 10, 770), formally the **Duke of Han** (韓公), was an eunuch official of the Chinese dynasty Tang Dynasty. He was powerful early during the reign of Emperor Daizong and was feared by others, including chancellors. At the urging of the chancellor Yuan Zai, Emperor Daizong secretly executed him at a meeting in 770, although Emperor Daizong publicly claimed that he committed suicide.

Background

Yu Chao'en was born in 722, during the reign of Emperor Xuanzong. His family was from Lu Prefecture (瀘州, in modern Luzhou, Sichuan). Late in Emperor Xuanzong's *Tianbao* (742–756) era, Yu was an eunuch attached to the examination bureau of government (門下省, *Menxia Sheng*). It was said that he was intelligent and was capable both in publicly announcing imperial edicts and in accounting.

During Emperor Suzong's reign

Early in the *Zhide* (756–758) era of Emperor Xuanzong's son and successor Emperor Suzong, during which Emperor Suzong was occupied with trying to suppress the rebel state Yan, Yu Chao'en was often commissioned to serve as a monitor of the armies, including serving as monitor of the army of Li Guangjin (李光進) during the recapturing of the capital Chang'an from Yan forces in 757. For his contributions to the campaign, he was put in charge of the eunuch bureau (內侍省, *Neishi Sheng*) and given a general title. Subsequently, after Tang forces recaptured the eastern capital Luoyang (which served as Yan's capital), forcing the Yan emperor An Qingxu to flee to Yecheng, nine Tang military governors (*Jiedushi*) put Yecheng under siege. The two most prominent generals of the nine were Guo Ziyi and Li Guangbi (Li Guangjin's brother), and as Emperor Suzong did not want to force one to submit to the command of the other, he did not commission a supreme commander; rather, he made Yu the monitor of the armies. It was said that Yu was jealous of Guo and often submitted reports criticizing Guo, but that Guo defused the tension by being humble with Yu.

In 759, the Yan general Shi Siming, who had briefly submitted to Tang but then rose again against Tang, attacked Tang forces at Yecheng and, while not achieving a victory, caused the Tang forces to collapse by themselves. He subsequently killed An Qingxu and took over the Yan throne. Meanwhile, Yu blamed the collapse on Guo, and as a result, Li Guangbi was put in command of the armies. Shi Siming subsequently attacked Luoyang and captured it. After a failed attempt by Tang forces to capture Luoyang, instigated by Yu and opposed by Li Guangbi, Shi tried to attack west toward Chang'an, but was repelled by the general Wei Boyu (衛伯玉), who was under Yu's command, at Shan Prefecture (陝州, in modern Sanmenxia, Henan). After a joint Tang and Huige army recaptured Luoyang in 762, Yu stationed his elite Shence Army to Bian Prefecture (汴州, in modern Kaifeng, Henan). For his contributions in this battle, he was created the Duke of Fengyi. Later in 762, he moved back to Shan Prefecture.

During Emperor Daizong's reign

Also in 762, Emperor Suzong died and was succeeded by his son Emperor Daizong. In 763, when Tufan launched a sudden attack against Chang'an, Emperor Daizong was forced to flee to Shan Prefecture. When he fled, very few imperial guard soldiers accompanied him, and it was not until Yu Chao'en met him at Huayin (華陰, in modern Weinan, Shaanxi) that he was protected by an army. Emperor Daizong gave Yu the title of monitor of troops over the entire realm (天下觀軍容宣慰處置使, *Tianxia Guanjunrong Xuanwei Chuzhishi*). After Emperor Xuanzong's return to Chang'an later in the year, Yu continued to be in command of the Shence Army and was greatly favored by Emperor Daizong, receiving much wealth. He was also permitted to enter and leave the palace as he wished. As the generals under his command continued to achieve important victories, particularly in the subsequent conflict against the rebellious general Pugu Huai'en, he considered himself capable in military command. As he considered himself learned in the Confucian classics as well and was capable of writing. In 765, during an attack by Pugu's forces, aligned with Huige and Tufan, Yu tried to use his soldiers to coerce the imperial officials into concurring with moving the capital to Hezhong (河中, in modern Yuncheng, Shanxi), but when an official named Liu publicly denounced the plan even with Yu's soldiers surrounding him, Yu abandoned the plan.

Also in 765, Yu, because he believed himself capable in literary matters, was made the acting principal of the imperial university (國子監, *Guozijian*). He was also created the Duke of Zheng. Under him, the imperial university, which had been destroyed during the Anshi Rebellion, was rebuilt. In 766, when the university's construction was completed, Yu personally lectured about the *I Ching*, tried to satirize the chancellors by talking about how a *ding* (a large cooking vessel often used to symbolize chancellorship) would overturn if imbalanced. The chancellor Wang Jin, was visibly incensed, but the more powerful Yuan Zai remained calm and pleasant, leading Yu to comment, "It is common for the target to get angry, but one who remains smiling needs to be paid attention to even more carefully." Yuan, however, was secretly resentful. Yu continued to be the principal of the university until 768, despite opposition by the official Chang Gun that a eunuch should not head the university.

In 767, Yu donated his mansion outside Chang'an to be rebuilt into a Buddhist temple dedicated to Emperor Daizong's deceased mother Consort Wu. As she was posthumously honored Empress Zhangjing, the temple was named Zhangjing Temple. The temple was said to be so luxuriously built that the wood in Chang'an was not enough, and several imperial pavilions had to be torn down so that the wood could be reused, and many officials and generals were required to donate their own houses for wood. In 768, he was created the Duke of Han. That year, at the anniversary of Consort Wu's death, Yu held a feast in her honor — at which he openly talked about how the chancellors were incompetent and should yield their seats. The chancellors did not dare to respond, but the junior officials Xiangli Zao (相里造) and Li Kan (李衎) responded and rebuked Yu, causing him to be displeased and to adjourn the feast early. Late in the year, Guo Ziyi's father's tomb was opened by grave robbers, but it was commonly believed that, because Yu disliked Guo immensely, that he was responsible for instigating it, and thus, when Guo subsequently arrived in the capital, there was anticipation that Guo would react violently. Guo defused the tension by stating that his soldiers have themselves robbed many graves, and that this must have been divine retribution. In 769, when Emperor Daizong had Yu escort Guo on a tour of Zhangjing Temple, Yuan tried to exploit the tension between the two by having Guo's subordinates falsely warning Guo that Yu was set to kill him during the tour. Guo refused to take precautions and told Yu about the rumors, defusing the tension between the two.

Meanwhile, several things caused Emperor Daizong to begin to be pleased with Yu. Yu was beginning to expect Emperor Daizong to accept every suggestion of his, and on one occasion, when Emperor Daizong did not, Yu stated, "Is there anything in this realm that I cannot decide?" Yu's young adoptive son Yu Linghui (魚令徽) was then serving as a eunuch inside the palace, and he wore the green robe for sixth and seventh rank officials. On an occasion, he had an argument with his colleagues, and he told Yu Chao'en about the argument. Yu Chao'en met Emperor Daizong the next day and stated, "My son's rank is too low, and his colleagues look down on him. Please let hi wear a purple robe." Even before Emperor Daizong could respond, the officials nearby, following Yu Chao'en's cue, already brought out a purple robe and put it on Yu Linghui. Yu Linghui bowed to thank Emperor Daizong, who smiled and responded, "This child now has a purple robe. He should be happy." However, he was internally displeased about how the incident went. Yuan saw that Emperor Daizong was becoming displeased with Yu, and therefore suggested to Emperor Daizong to eliminate Yu. They began to plot together. Yuan began to bribe two close associates of Yu's; Zhou Hao (周皓) the commander of the imperial guard archery corps, and Huangfu Wen (皇甫溫) the military governor of Shan Circuit (headquartered in modern Sanmenxia). Zhou and Huangfu became associates of Yuan's, and from this point on, Yuan and Emperor Daizong were able to anticipate Yu's moves.

In spring 770, at Yuan's suggestion, Emperor Daizong carried out several moves that were intending to be preludes to eliminating Yu — moving the general Li Baoyu from being the military governor (*Jiedushi*) of Fengxiang Circuit (鳳翔, headquartered in modern Baoji) to Shannan West Circuit (山南西道, headquartered in modern Xi'an, Shaanxi, to the southwest of Chang'an), while moving Huangfu, then the military governor of Shan Circuit (headquartered in modern Sanmenxia) to Fengxiang — while allaying Yu's suspicions by transferring control of four counties near Chang'an to the imperial guards, under Yu's command. (Yuan's intent was that, as Huangfu arrived in Chang'an, to use his soldiers against Yu.) Soon, when Huangfu arrived in Chang'an, Yuan laid a trap for Yu with Huangfu's and Zhou's soldiers, and at a secret meeting between Emperor Daizong and Yu, Yuan and Emperor Daizong acted and killed Yu. Emperor Daizong then issued a public rebuke of Yu and then claimed that, when Yu received the rebuke, he committed suicide. Emperor Daizong still had him buried with honors, at imperial expense. Source (edited): "http://en.wikipedia.org/wiki/Yu_Chao%27en"

Zhu Jingmei

Zhu Jingmei (朱敬玫) (d. 885) was an eunuch late in the Tang Dynasty who, after killing Duan Yanmo the military governor (*Jiedushi*) of Jingnan Circuit (荊南, headquartered in modern Jingzhou, Hubei), became the effective ruling authority for the circuit due to his command of the elite Zhongyong Army (忠勇軍). In 885, however, he was assassinated by Zhang Gui, who had just forcibly seized the circuit after arresting the Zhu-appointed military governor Chen Ru.

Conflict with Duan Yanmo and takeover of circuit

Little is known about Zhu Jingmei's background, because, although the official histories of Tang Dynasty, the *Book of Tang* and the *New Book of Tang*, both contained collections of biographies for prominent eunuchs, neither collection contained a biography for Zhu. What is known is that Zhu became the eunuch monitor of the army at Jingnan Circuit sometime in or after 880 (when Yang Fuguang was still the eunuch monitor at Jingnan) and in or before 882.

After Zhu took up his position as eunuch monitor at Jingnan, he organized a group of 3,000 elite soldiers into a Zhongyong Army (忠勇軍), under his own command. He also got into conflicts with the military governor Duan Yanmo, and Duan planned to kill him. Zhu preemptively acted and, in 882, attacked and killed Duan. He then made the deputy mayor of Jingnan's capital Jiangling Municipality (江陵) acting military governor. Then-reigning Emperor Xizong (who was then at Chengdu after the imperial capital Chang'an had fallen to the major agrarian rebel Huang Chao), hearing what happened, commissioned the imperial official Zheng Shaoye (鄭紹業), who had previously served as military governor of Jingnan, as military governor. However, Zheng was fearful of Zhu and did not report to Jingnan. Zhu thereafter made the officer Chen Ru acting military governor, a commission that Emperor Xizong subsequently confirmed; yet later in 884, Emperor Xizong made Chen military governor. It was said that while Zhu was in control of Jingnan, he found excuses to slaughter many officers and merchants and seize their wealths, making himself very wealthy. At one point, when Emperor Xizong tried to recall him and replace him with Yang Xuanhui (楊玄晦), he refused to be recalled and settled down in Jiangling.

Death

In 885, Chen Ru, while having been commissioned by Zhu, became weary of the lack of discipline the Zhongyong Army showed, and decided to take action. Previously, when Zheng Shaoye was military governor, he had put the officer Shentu Cong (申屠琮) in command of a group of soldiers to serve in the campaign against Huang Chao. When Shentu and his soldiers returned to Jingnan in 885, Chen informed Shentu of the situation and ordered him to destroy the Zhongyong Army. When the Zhongyong officer Cheng Junzhi (程君之) found out, he tried to take his soldiers and flee to Lang Prefecture (朗州, in modern Changde, Hunan). Shentu pursued and attacked him, killing more than 100 Zhongyong soldiers on the way and causing the rest to scatter. Shentu thereafter became briefly dominant in the Jingnan Circuit government. Soon thereafter, though, when Chen tried to induce two army officers from Huainan Circuit (淮南, headquartered in modern Yangzhou, Jiangsu) — Zhang Gui and Han Shide (韓師德) — to attack the prefect of Lang, Lei Man, who had been repeatedly pillaging the region, Zhang not only did not attack Lei, but instead attacked Jiangling and expelled Chen. Chen tried to flee to Emperor Xizong's court at Chengdu, but Zhang intercepted him and put him under arrest in Jiangling. Thereafter, Zhang became aware of the wealth that Zhu Jingmei had accumulated, and therefore sent soldiers to kill Zhu at his mansion at night and seize Zhu's wealth. Source (edited): "http://en.wikipedia.org/wiki/Zhu_Jingmei"